HEADS UP

CHANGING MINDS ON
MENTAL HEALTH

HEADS

CHANGING MINDS ON MENTAL HEALTH

UP

MELANIE SIEBERT

ILLUSTRATIONS BY
BELLE WUTHRICH

ORCA BOOK PUBLISHERS

Library and Archives Canada Cataloguing in Publication

Title: Heads up: changing minds on mental health / Melanie Siebert ;
illustrations by Belle Wuthrich.
Names: Siebert, Melanie, author. | Wuthrich, Belle, 1989- illustrator.
Series: Orca issues.
Description: Series statement: Orca issues | Includes bibliographical references and index.
Identifiers: Canadiana (print) 20190226226 | Canadiana (ebook) 20190226269 |
ISBN 9781459819115 (softcover) | ISBN 9781459819122 (PDF) | ISBN 9781459819139 (EPUB)
Subjects: LCSH: Mental health—Juvenile literature. | LCSH: Teenagers—Mental health—Juvenile
literature. | LCSH: Well-being—Juvenile literature. | LCSH: Adolescent psychology—Juvenile literature.
Classification: LCC RJ503 .S54 2020 | DDC j616.8900835—dc23

Library of Congress Control Number: 2019954271
Simultaneously published in Canada and the United States in 2020

Summary: This nonfiction book for teen readers is a guide to understanding and coping
with mental health, mental illness, trauma and recovery. It features real-life stories of
resilient teens and highlights innovative approaches to mental health challenges.

*Orca Book Publishers is committed to reducing the consumption of nonrenewable resources in the making
of our books. We make every effort to use materials that support a sustainable future.*

Orca Book Publishers gratefully acknowledges the support for its publishing programs provided
by the following agencies: the Government of Canada, the Canada Council for the Arts and the
Province of British Columbia through the BC Arts Council and the Book Publishing Tax Credit.

Edited by Sarah N. Harvey
Design by Belle Wuthrich
Cover and interior illustrations by Belle Wuthrich

ORCA BOOK PUBLISHERS
orcabook.com

Printed and bound in China.

23 22 21 20   •   4 3 2 1

TO NICK, JULIA, GRACE, RACHEL, JESSE AND MICAH
IN MEMORY OF JOSH

CONTENTS

INTRODUCTION

I WANT TO TELL YOU A STORY. I hadn't heard from Tina in a while, so when she called and asked me to meet her at McDonald's, I jumped at the chance. It was late at night. I wanted to buy her something to eat, but she wouldn't let me. Tina was wearing a tutu and layers of sweaters and hoodies topped with a hockey jersey. She waved her arms and rattled a stream of disconnected thoughts on the FBI, diamond jewelry and salvation, then ordered an extra-large coffee. The server was polite and smiling, and I was relieved that she treated Tina kindly.

Tina's stare was intense and darting. She sussed out the tables warily, then picked one. She was edgy about cameras recording us. She kept telling me to keep my voice down. She should be paid $1,000 an hour to model, she said. People were breaking into her apartment. A famous singer was in love with her and his new hit song was written for her. When I questioned something, she flared into anger, pointed her finger at me. "I know!" she said. "I have the mind of God." I was tense. I didn't know what to say. I knew she wasn't eating. She wasn't sleeping. She wasn't working. She kept thinking people were out to hurt her. She was suffering, and it broke my heart.

Tina is someone I love who has been diagnosed with a mental illness. She is also one of the most generous, thoughtful, intelligent and kind people I know. When she's feeling better, she strikes up lively, warm conversations with strangers. She attracts a mob of kids wherever she goes and loves to blow bubbles or do magic tricks. She surprises people with delightful, zany gifts. But sometimes her thoughts don't match reality. Sometimes her feelings come out in intense waves. I'm pretty sure the famous singer isn't in love with her and no one is breaking into her apartment. And yet her feelings of elation and fear are absolutely real.

When Tina first started struggling, it was very confusing for me. Her thoughts seemed disconnected from reality. I didn't understand. And I didn't know how to help her.

I was also having my own troubles. I'd find myself biking to university day after day, crying while I rode but not knowing why. Soon nothing was fun anymore. I just wanted to lie in bed and never get up. Concentrating and getting my work done was a struggle. On the outside, I could often fake it, but on the inside, it felt like I was shriveling up. I didn't know where to get help, and I certainly didn't want to tell anyone what I was going through because I felt like such a failure. I didn't know how to help myself either.

Eventually I talked to a counselor. And slowly I started opening up to people in my life. Turns out I wasn't the only one feeling strange and alone. The more I talked about what I was going through, the more I found that other people had similar experiences and understood my confusion and pain.

We all go through tough times. This is human. Distress sometimes even helps us to change and grow. But just as we all need to learn to take care of our physical health, we also need to learn to take care of our *mental health* in order to cope with troubles and enjoy life.

Things get trickier when distress gets so intense that it's difficult to function in daily life, or when it goes on so long that it seems never-ending. We often call this a *mental illness* or *mental disorder*. Between health and illness there is a wide range of experiences, and most often people don't fit neatly into any box or diagnosis. That's why I want to tell you a bunch of stories that illustrate how each person's struggle and journey to wellness is unique and personal.

Some people's troubles are expressed outwardly, in words and actions that might seem odd or big and emotional. Other people keep things more hidden and suffer in silence. Either way, it can be very difficult and confusing—both for the person who is struggling and for their loved ones. And yet I believe there is hope for all of us to find peace, belonging and a meaningful life.

I work now as a youth and family counselor. Each day, young people sit with me and talk about what's up. They tell me about what sucks in their lives, sometimes ranting, sometimes barely able to get

"Just as we all need to learn to take care of our physical health, we also need to learn to take care of our mental health."

MELANIE SIEBERT

a word out. It's all okay. My office is a place where I hope people can just be themselves. To do that, they have to feel safe. So that's my job—to be present, calm and accepting, so that each person can freely speak from their heart.

I wish I could tell you some of these stories, because the youth I see inspire me every single day with their strength, honesty and courage. But I've made a serious promise to each of them that I'll keep their stories private. So in this book I only tell stories I've lived and stories from my friends, family and people I've interviewed who gave me permission to tell their stories, sometimes after I've promised to change their name to protect their privacy.

Science can tell us a lot about how our brains work and why we feel and think the way we do. For each one of us, our sense of well-being is affected by the body we were born with, the good and bad things that have happened to us and the choices we make. To feel happy and well, we all need healthy food, a safe place to live and a sense of belonging. When people are bullied or discriminated against or made to feel like they don't matter, it hurts their mental health.

"Mental" might make it sound like it's all in our heads. I think it's more than that. When we're in distress, our bodies, our emotions, our thoughts and our spirits are involved. In fact, the word *psyche*— which is part of the words *psychology* and *psychiatry*—comes from a Greek word that means "the breath of life." *Psyche* refers to that most mysterious thing that makes each person a one-of-a-kind living being. That's what we're talking about here—what happens when our living being gets injured. It's not just in your head. This is core stuff! It's not simple or easy. And there is still a lot we don't know about why people suffer from emotional pain and distress. So hang on as we explore both what we know and what we don't know, the theories and the mysteries. The stories in this book will show you there's hope for anyone who's struggling.

1

MENTAL HEALTH

THE SCIENCE, THEORIES AND MYSTERIES

SUFFERING HAS ALWAYS been a part of being human. Philosophers, shamans, priests, artists, scientists, doctors and *therapists* have all tried to understand it. Throughout history, people have tried to figure out how to get through it. How to make it better. No life is pain-free. Everybody hurts.

While some pain is clearly physical—like the pain from a twisted ankle—pain is often thought of as being emotional, psychological and even spiritual. It hurts when someone says something mean. It hurts when no one understands. It hurts when you've let yourself or someone else down. Sometimes suffering comes in the form of sadness, worry or anger. Sometimes it's self-hatred or shame. Sometimes it's racing thoughts or an ache in your chest or a dead feeling inside. Sometimes it's pain there just isn't words for.

It's scary to think that it's possible to lose control of your thoughts and emotions, to lose all sense of what's real and what's not. Or to be so anguished that you no longer feel like yourself. Or to be in such immense pain that it seems almost impossible to go on living. This is serious stuff.

WHAT IS MENTAL HEALTH? WHAT IS MENTAL ILLNESS?

ood mental health is the ability to enjoy the good things in life and cope with the difficult things. It's the ability to adapt and change. And to balance stress and relaxation. Good mental health doesn't mean the absence of struggles; it means being able to deal with things and still take care of yourself and your relationships.

Everybody has ups and downs. Everybody has thoughts and feelings that sometimes are overwhelming or distressing. So what is mental illness? When does regular old sadness tip into depression? When does a burst of energy and creativity become manic? When do worries morph into an anxiety disorder? When do odd beliefs become delusional or psychotic?

Mental illness and *mental disorder* are terms often used to describe when a person's thoughts and feelings are messed up to the point that it is difficult for them to function in regular life. A mental illness or disorder—like **anxiety**, **depression**, **schizophrenia** or **post-traumatic stress disorder (PTSD)**—is a label that's attached to a cluster of symptoms that cause a person great distress. The symptoms can include major changes in a person's thoughts, perceptions, emotions, and behaviors. To qualify as an illness or disorder, these symptoms are

usually serious enough that the person has difficulty taking care of themselves or relating to others.

The World Health Organization names mental disorders as one of the top causes of poor health and disability. Keep in mind, though, that many mental health issues are temporary and resolve with time and good self-care.

The terms *mental health*, *mental illness* and *mental disorder* all come from a medical perspective that tends to focus on the brain as the source of the problem. This brings up some questions: Is what we're talking about really mental? I mean, is it all in our heads? And is what we're talking about truly illness? Is it a disease or defect in the brain? Is it something wrong inside an individual person? Or is it more complicated than that?

As you'll see in this book, people have different takes on this. Cultures have different takes on this. And through time, understandings have shifted.

We're going to look at some of the different ways of making sense of mental health. Biomedical explanations focus on genetics and the brain's circuitry and chemicals. This approach relies on science to provide insight into what is out of whack in our brains, so that we can develop treatments, as we have for other illnesses. We'll also look at psychosocial explanations, which focus more on how people's wellness is affected by inequality, discrimination, violence, poverty and other social problems. This approach emphasizes the need for society to change in order for people to be healthy and happy. We'll look at **Indigenous** perspectives that offer a more holistic approach, where wellness is about balancing mind, body, heart and spirit. In this view, a person's wellbeing is interconnected with their family, community, culture and land. We'll also consider a trauma-informed approach, one that emphasizes how trauma—really scary, overwhelming experiences—can affect our whole body and sense of self.

Each of these approaches to understanding mental health can open up different possibilities for sparking change in ourselves and in our world.

SHAWN'S STORY

op-U-lar! Pop-U-lar! Shawn Glynn Pendenque rode high on a Toronto Pride Parade float pumping out his hit single, "Popular." The crowd pulsed to the electro-dance groove he lay down. "They know who you are because you're popular!" he sang.

Back then, Shawn looked the part of a magnetic Black pop star. His music career was ramping up. He had an education and a day job as a youth counselor. He owned a house and a car. But underneath all that success, Shawn says, "I was totally messed up."

Shawn had worked with youth for over a decade. At some point the number of Black youths he saw going to jail started to really

Shawn Glynn Pendenque

bother him. The bruises and wounds he saw on their bodies made his stomach knot. Anger started to boil. "I felt I had to be a savior for these kids," Shawn says.

Looking back, Shawn sees that he slowly started becoming delusional. He started to think he was an angel sent to save these kids. He heard voices from heaven. He believed he was Jesus. For weeks, he didn't sleep. Sometimes he'd roam the streets, muttering, raging. Night after night, he worked frantically on a twenty-seven-page manifesto declaring that court judges were all going to burn in hell.

Shortly after Shawn sent his manifesto to the judges, cops raided his house and arrested him for uttering death threats. Shawn was characterized as a religious extremist and imprisoned. No one realized he was having a mental health crisis and needed help. In prison the symptoms of *psychosis* got worse and worse until he lost all touch with reality. Eventually he was diagnosed with *schizoaffective disorder*, a condition that includes major mood symptoms along with *hallucinations* and *delusions*.

"I lost absolutely everything," Shawn says, "my home, my car, my record label, my professional identity." When he was released from prison, he had nowhere to go. He turned to Loft, a nonprofit organization in Toronto that supports people with mental health and *addictions* challenges. Given a stable home, Shawn started to work on his recovery.

We'll pick up Shawn's story again later, but first let's take a closer look at the brain, so we can begin to understand what goes on inside our heads.

FANTASTIC PLASTIC
CIRCUITS, CHEMICALS AND THE SCIENCE OF CHANGING BRAINS

he brain is such a delicate, Jell-O-y glob. On YouTube, I watch a neurobiologist hold a shiny pink brain in her latex-gloved hands, caressing its plump worm-like texture. It's eerie and marvelous to think that this fragile thing once floated in someone's skull, processing sights, sounds, thoughts, feelings—a whole world of experience.

Science has focused on the brain as the center of operations, the key to understanding our emotions and behavior. And yet, as scientist Emerson M. Pugh once said, "If the brain were so simple that we could understand it, we would be so simple that we couldn't."

The brain is an incredible mass of about 100 billion nerve cells called neurons. Every action or emotion creates a pathway in your brain, a trail laid down by one brain cell releasing a chemical and the next cell absorbing it and sending it on down the line. These chemical messengers are called *neurotransmitters*. Each skateboard trick or math problem lights up a precise path in the brain. And every time you repeat an action or a thought, that pathway is strengthened. If you have learned to play a guitar riff or sink a basketball, you know how it starts off feeling awkward and clumsy, but as you keep practicing, eventually you can do it without thinking—well, obviously you're still thinking, but it's effortless. Here's what happens: "neurons that fire together, wire together."

Scientists used to think that the majority of the brain's development happened in early childhood and that, after that, things got pretty static. Now we know that the human brain is incredibly plastic. *Plasticity* refers to the ability of something to be easily shaped or molded. In this case, neuroplasticity means that the brain has the ability to change and grow throughout a person's life. This is good news—it means we can work to heal our brains. If you light up the pathways that make you feel good and calm, those pathways get strengthened.

"If the brain were so simple that we could understand it, we would be so simple that we couldn't."

EMERSON M. PUGH

JUST A CHEMICAL IMBALANCE?

The science of neurotransmitters has helped us understand that mental illnesses are linked to chemical imbalances. Over 100 neurotransmitters have been identified. The psychiatric medications we now use to treat things like depression or schizophrenia work by blocking, stimulating or mimicking these chemicals. In Canada, psychiatric medications are the most prescribed drugs other than cardiovascular (heart) medications.

Even though medications don't work for everyone, they can provide relief from the symptoms of mental illness. For Shawn, medications helped him calm his emotions and get on with living.

Each person has a unique factory for producing the chemicals of consciousness. This factory may have production glitches related to the biology you're born with. But mental illness isn't necessarily just a chemical imbalance. Life causes chemical imbalances. Everything from grief to violence to hunger to bullying can mess with our chemical balance. Positive experiences like a comforting hug, a sunset or a hard run can produce happy chemicals. Factory settings might be skewed, but that's usually not the whole story. Sometimes we've got to work on fixing life in order to get the good chemicals flowing.

THE EMOTIONAL BRAIN

The main job of a brain is to ensure survival. The emotional part of the brain is built to react to danger in order to keep us safe. Recently, machines have been invented that can watch the brain in action. PET scans and fMRIs allow scientists to track what happens in the brain when a person meditates or is given a mouthful of sugar or is reminded of a violent attack they once experienced.

The most basic part of the brain, the part that first develops in the womb, is the **brain stem**. Sometimes it's called the reptilian brain because it is as ancient and simple as a snake's brain. The brain stem controls the vital functions of breathing, body temperature and heart rate.

The **limbic brain** records memories and whether they were pleasant or unpleasant. It's called the mammalian brain because it's something that all social mammals have. This is where emotions are sparked. The limbic brain judges what is dangerous or safe, pleasurable or painful.

Together, the reptilian brain and the mammalian brain can be thought of as the **emotional brain**. The emotional brain is in charge of survival. It's fast and instinctive. It lights up for sugar. It freaks at danger. Even a memory of something bad can get the emotional brain revving with fear.

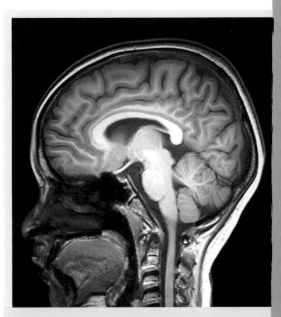

The emotional brain sends signals of danger or safety to the body. The thinking brain can help us understand and respond to these signals. But big emotions can overwhelm our ability to think clearly.

THE THINKING BRAIN

The **neocortex**—often called the thinking brain—is in charge of logic, imagination, planning and control. It figures out how things work, weighs pros and cons and makes decisions. Other mammals also have

17

When we feel calm and safe, we are better at making good decisions and connecting with others.

a neocortex, but in humans it's thicker and more developed. The neocortex is the command center where we decode language, store information and generate meaning.

It's the thinking brain that allows us to regulate our emotions and hold off on impulses so we can consider our options and predict consequences. It helps us to take a second and not say or do something hurtful. It helps us resist a piece of cake or punch a pillow instead of a person.

It's also the part of the brain that lets us tune in to another person and understand their experience. In other words, it helps us to be compassionate and socially connected. The thinking brain helps us to act wisely and develop caring relationships.

Since the emotional brain reacts with lightning-fast reflexes, the thinking brain is pretty much always playing catch-up. If you round a corner and encounter a stranger in a dark alley, your body will react before you have time to think about who they are or why you're scared. The emotional brain can trigger the whole body into *fight, flight or freeze* (see more on p. 22) before you can even think. It takes time for the thinking brain to catch up and make sense of the experience.

NEUROSCIENTIST PAUL D. MACLEAN said the relationship between the thinking brain and the emotional brain is like the relationship between a rider and a horse. The emotional brain is like a horse that is spirited and a bit hard to control. But if the rider is skilled, and the weather and terrain aren't too tricky, it's a pretty smooth ride. If something spooks the horse, though, the rider can be thrown— or left hanging on for dear life until the horse runs out of steam.

To get along in life, we need the energy and instincts of the emotional brain. But we also need the thinking brain to be a good and skilled rider in order for us to make wise decisions.

Paul D. MacLean

IT'S NOT ALL IN YOUR HEAD

THE BODY/BRAIN CONNECTION

E*ver felt anger* exploding in your chest? Felt sadness crushing in? Felt checked out and absent from your body? Or ever heard these expressions: *My heart sank! I was scared stiff! I almost lost my shit! That made my skin crawl! My gut said no!*

Charles Darwin, the biologist who developed the theory of evolution, noticed that when it comes to emotions, we're a lot like other animals. The hair stands up on the back of our necks. We clench our jaws. In anger, we can get big, swaggery and in your face.

In despair, our shoulders can collapse as our head bows, or maybe we curl right up into a ball. In fear, we get shaky and ready to bolt.

Emotions aren't just in our heads. They inhabit the body. They activate our muscles and animate our faces. They communicate to others. And they motivate and shape our actions. As Darwin observed, our emotions are essential to survival—they propel us to seek safety, to take care of our needs and to bond with others who can help us survive.

Illustration of a terrified cat from Charles Darwin's The Expression of the Emotions in Man and Animals *(1872).*

As social animals, we pay a ton of attention to the people around us in order to survive. We can sense the slightest shifts in another person's mood, tuning in to changes in their forehead creases, eye movement, mouth shape, shoulder tension and posture. In turn, our body responds with its own physical signals.

When we're doing well, there's a balanced relationship between emotions and thinking. Our feelings are vibrant and give us good information about what feels safe and pleasurable and what doesn't. And yet our thinking is still in control, and we're able to evaluate the emotional information and make good choices.

If emotions get super intense, it can feel like your chest is caving in, you're suffocating or your body is a helpless rag. In this state, it's hard to think clearly. It's no wonder people often feel driven to do just about anything to get the horrible feeling to go away. Some turn to a dark room. Some to the adrenaline rush of speeding on the highway. Others turn to drugs or sex or *self-injury* to either numb the feelings or block out pain with completely different intense feelings.

THE SUPERPOWERS OF FIGHT, FLIGHT OR FREEZE

The nervous system is the body's major communication network. It essentially has two parts: a gas pedal and a brake pedal. The gas pedal is the sympathetic nervous system—the part that revs the body up for action by speeding up the heart and increasing blood pressure. The brake pedal is the parasympathetic nervous system, which slows the body down, preparing it to feed and breed, and to rest and digest. The body has the incredible ability to regulate the flow of energy required with second-by-second, play-by-play precision. When we sense danger, the body revs up into survival mode. On the flip side, when we feel safe and nourished, we go into relaxation mode. This is important, because it's when the body heals and recovers.

The amygdala, part of the emotional brain, is a sensitive alarm system that detects threats. To warn us of danger, the amygdala activates the sympathetic nervous system to create the body's fight-or-flight response. Stress hormones surge through your body, pumping up your heart rate, blood pressure and breathing. This is the body's brilliant way of sending more oxygen to your muscles as it gets ready to fight for your life or flee to safety. Fight or flight gives you an instant charge of emergency energy.

If the threat seems overwhelming, though, the body can go into a freeze response. It can feel like you're paralyzed and your mind is blank. When an animal feels cornered by a predator, the freeze response is a last-ditch effort to survive. It's like playing dead in the hope that the predator will leave you alone. In extreme situations, blood pressure drops, muscles go limp and painkillers flood in. In car accidents, rapes and other violent assaults, survivors often feel like they've left their bodies. A person may feel no pain or even have no specific memories of what happened. The body goes into a highly protective state that allows it to endure the unimaginable.

The ability to regulate your emotions and feel safe and calm in your body is a big part of mental health.

BIG HITS
HOW TRAUMA TRIPS US UP

Trauma is a response to any frightening experience that overwhelms a person's ability to handle it. Traumatic events include violence, abuse, neglect, accidents and sudden loss, or any other experience that makes you feel helpless and out of control. Trauma puts our bodies into survival mode. Our body's response to trauma can last for days, months or even years.

Shawn tells me that when he was having delusions that he was sent as a divine savior, he was also having intense nightmares of his own abuse. He was having flashbacks and trying to shut out bad memories. He felt physical pain in places on his body where he had been beaten as a child.

When I ask Shawn about the connection between his mental health struggles and earlier experiences of trauma, he says that no professional has ever asked him about this. "No one?" I ask. "No one," he says. In all his appointments with doctors and psychiatrists, no one ever asked about his history of trauma. But Shawn has thought about the connection. He now realizes that when he was working with youth in the courts, what he saw and heard was triggering his own trauma response.

TRAUMA RESPONSE

Live-action brain scans show that when the emotional brain is in fight, flight or freeze, the thinking brain shuts down. In this survival mode, language and logic are left behind. Trauma experts have noted that this explains why people who have experienced horrible events have trouble putting them into words. Or if they do try to, they often end up feeling like the story just doesn't capture the experience. And yet these traumatic experiences can return as vivid flashbacks, nightmares or stress bursts that seem to come out of the blue.

Trauma triggers can be anything that reminds a person of a past trauma—a scent, texture, sound, place or any other reminder—and kick-starts a stress response. For example, when Shawn saw bruises or cuts on the bodies of his young clients, he'd start to feel panicky.

Flashbacks replay the trauma as if it were happening all over again. The person's body responds with intense reactions as if in actual danger. In fact, the person may not even be able to realize

TRAUMA
IS AN
INJURY
THAT CAN
BE HEALED.

that it's a memory. They are just rattled, terrified, exploding or completely frozen.

Many people who have experienced trauma are either perpetually keyed up and on edge or are numb and checked out. Both are the result of the nervous system being overwhelmed. When your alarm system is constantly going off or has been muted, you no longer have a reliable way to judge what is safe and what isn't.

For survivors of trauma, even when there is no real danger, it can feel like danger lurks everywhere. Living with a constantly activated nervous system means even regular activities, like going out for dinner or going to school, might feel too stimulating. It can also be difficult to talk to a doctor or counselor.

On the other hand, sometimes people who are used to being in constant danger find it hard to be in a calm, quiet environment because it doesn't match how wired they feel. For survivors it's often difficult to enjoy life because they are so focused on controlling intense physical reactions. It makes sense that many survivors turn to alcohol, drugs and self-injury. But as Shawn's story will show, there are ways to heal trauma and find well-being.

SHAWN'S STORY CONTINUED

When Shawn was 16, his father dropped him off at a youth shelter with his things in a garbage bag. Shawn drifted from shelter to shelter, lonely, frightened and struggling to find food, warmth and safety. He learned to be a hustler, selling sex in order to survive. He started using drugs to numb the constant, unbearable pain. Life was chaotic, and there was no one to trust.

"My father hated me for being gay," Shawn says. "He couldn't stand to breathe the same air I breathed." Although his family was respected in their church and community, Shawn says what had happened behind closed doors was abuse.

"After that, I put myself in so much danger," Shawn says, "because I didn't love myself at all." He attempted suicide twice.

THE TROUBLING STATS

MANY CHILDREN EXPERIENCE abuse or witness violence. Some children don't have their basic needs for food, clothing and safety met. Many more experience emotional neglect, meaning they are not given the affection and care from adults that they need to be healthy.

Being neglected or abused increases the likelihood that a person will experience difficulty in school, social problems, poverty and further violence. Living with consistently elevated levels of stress can also lead to problems with mood, memory, concentration and sleep. And the more difficult experiences a child has, the higher their risk for major health problems—everything from heart, liver and lung diseases to mental health problems, alcohol and drug use and suicide. Researchers have even found a strong link between childhood trauma and experiencing hallucinations as an adult.

More than half the people who use mental health services have been abused or neglected or have witnessed violence as children. People are frequently diagnosed with depression, anxiety or a **substance use disorder**, but the underlying cause—trauma—is rarely acknowledged or treated. In mental health services, we need more professionals who understand trauma and have the skills to help people heal.

2 in 3 people reported at least 1 ACE

1 in 8 people reported 4+ ACEs

Somehow, though, he still believed in something greater than himself and this kept him going. He'd hunt out pianos in churches and community centers and ask God to teach him how to play.

Shawn says it's difficult to make peace with a mental health diagnosis. He knows he needs to take his medications to maintain a level of balance. But he also tells the people he now works with that there are other ways to create balance and wellness.

A big part of Shawn's work as a counselor is just listening to people's stories. This can relieve the burden of carrying the story alone. One of the most helpful things in Shawn's own recovery was attending a group for men who have survived *sexualized abuse*. For the first time, he felt safe enough to share his painful story.

"Dealing with shame," Shawn says, "was my big thing." He was ashamed of being gay, of having been abused and of having a mental illness. But when the group honored his story, he started to realize that it wasn't his fault and began to recognize his own courage. Having other people who believe you and see your strength— whether a therapy group, a counselor or a friend—is healing.

PEOPLE WITH 4+ ACES

2 x
more likely to develop
heart disease or cancer

4 x
more likely to develop lung disease

4.5 x
more likely to experience depression

5 x
more likely to use street drugs

7 x
more likely to have a drinking problem

10 x
more likely to have injected drugs

12 x
more likely to attempt suicide

ACES

ADVERSE CHILDHOOD EXPERIENCES, or ACEs, are difficult or traumatic things that happen in childhood and can affect a person throughout life.

NEGLECT
- Physical needs not met
- Emotional needs not met

ABUSE
- Physical
- Emotional
- Sexualized

OTHER DIFFICULT STUFF AT HOME
- Parents separated or divorced
- Violence between others
- Substance abuse
- Family member mentally ill
- Family member in jail

DISRUPT BRAIN DEVELOPMENT

↓

MAKE IT MORE DIFFICULT TO LEARN THINGS (including how to manage emotions and create healthy relationships)

↓

MORE LIKELY TO USE UNHEALTHY WAYS OF COPING

↓

MORE LIKELY TO DEVELOP HEALTH AND SOCIAL PROBLEMS

↓

MORE LIKELY TO DIE EARLY

Based on the Adverse Childhood Experiences study (1995–1997), a major American study by the Centers for Disease Control and Prevention and Kaiser Permanente, that collected data from over 17,000 people.

"SOME KIDS LIVE WITH MORE STRESS AND UNCERTAINTY AND LESS SAFETY AND BELONGING. THEY GET MESSAGES THAT IMPLY 'YOU'RE NOT GOOD ENOUGH,' 'YOU DON'T MATTER' AND 'THE WORLD IS A SCARY PLACE.'"

"It's real. It's true," Shawn says. "It happened and I can't change that." That's the first step toward acceptance. "The next step," he says, "is developing a safety plan for myself. When I'm triggered, by smells, thoughts, holidays, dreams, places—whatever—what am I going to do?"

Shawn brings a supportive person with him to family events. Or sometimes he chooses to stay away and send a card instead. He continues to draw strength from the teachings of Jesus and is working on forgiving his father. He keeps a dream journal and talks about his dreams with someone he trusts the next day. He spends time with people he finds calm and peaceful.

Just like when he was a teenager, Shawn turns to music and songwriting. When he plays the piano, rich chords fill the room and his voice delicately glides into falsetto. The songs release some of the pain and share his dream of a gentler, kinder world.

LIVING IN A MESSED-UP WORLD

While troubles like anxiety or depression might seem to be individual illnesses, the problem is often in society. Racism, homophobia, transphobia, ableism and other forms of oppression take a big toll on a person's wellbeing. People who are *LGBTQ2S+*, Indigenous, racialized, disabled or are marginalized in other ways are often targeted individually and face systemic inequality. When people have to deal with prejudice and discrimination, these repeated stressful or traumatic experiences affect their physical and mental health. If we feel ignored or disrespected or bullied, feelings of calm and safety vanish. If we're not safe or accepted, our nervous system can slide into anxiety, irritability or numbness and disconnection.

Social problems can affect families too. If parents are highly stressed—because of things like poverty, racism or their own trauma

LIVING IN POVERTY often leads to mental health struggles. And the reverse is true too: living with mental health struggles often leads to poverty. Poverty means more than not having enough money to meet your needs. Poverty is a tangled web of troubles causing more troubles. Think of what Shawn went through (p. 12): surviving on cheap food, living in unsafe conditions, not being able to find good work, constantly worrying about what tomorrow might bring. All these can create immense stress and health problems, which can then lead to depression or anxiety, which make it next to impossible to go to school or work or even get help. One thing leads to the next, and things spiral downward.

According to the World Health Organization, people who experience hunger, face mounting debts, or live in poor or overcrowded housing are much more likely to face mental health struggles. Overall, people who live in poverty are twice as likely to suffer from a diagnosable mental illness. And they are eight times more likely to be living with schizophrenia than those who are well off. Fighting poverty and inequality is an important way of improving mental health.

"Poverty is almost certainly the biggest determinant of health in our society," says Dr. Gary Bloch, a family doctor at St. Michael's Hospital in Toronto. Dr. Bloch often applies for social assistance, bus passes or money for food on behalf of his patients.

history—it might make it hard for them to consistently be present and comforting for their kids. They might feel distant or distracted. Or they might lash out because they are in their own fight-or-flight mode. This can be really hard on kids. If you can't get consistent comfort and protection from your main caregivers, the world can begin to feel unsafe and unpredictable.

No parents are perfect. I'm not trying to blame parents here. Usually parents are doing their best. But sometimes parents need support to heal from their own trauma and mental health problems. And if you're a kid, that shouldn't be your job. Ideally, adults will turn to a counselor, doctor, spiritual leader or friend for help.

Throughout life, but particularly when we're young, the messages we get from our world can get inside our heads. Some kids live in safety and get big doses of acceptance and nurturing. They get the messages "you're okay," "you're worth loving" and "the world is a safe place." Some kids live with more stress and uncertainty and less safety and belonging. They get messages that imply "you're not good enough," "you don't matter" and "the world is a scary place." These messages come to us through the ways people treat us, but also through movies, social media and all the ways we're included or excluded in society. They shape how we think about ourselves and can have a big impact on mental health.

INTERGENERATIONAL TRAUMA

In 2012 I went with a friend of mine who is Kwakwaka'wakw (from coastal British Columbia) to the Truth and Reconciliation Commission (TRC) hearings in Victoria, British Columbia. These hearings happened all over Canada and gave survivors of Indian residential schools an opportunity to speak about how their lives had been impacted by the abuse they suffered.

My friend gave her testimony about how her experiences at Indian residential school had filled her with fear, anger and shame. As I sat in the large hotel conference room and listened, with wads of damp tissue in my hands, person after person told their story. All the tissues used to wipe our tears were collected in paper bags that were then respectfully burned in a sacred fire.

For over 150 years, Indigenous children were ripped away from their families and forced to attend Indian residential schools. These schools, supported by the Canadian government and usually run by churches, were intended to "kill the Indian in the child." Children were robbed of the love and security of their families. They were forbidden to speak their own languages. Many children experienced physical, emotional and sexualized abuse. And many did not survive. The TRC called Canada's policies cultural genocide—the systematic attempt to destroy Indigenous values and cultural identity.

For many Indigenous people, their personal healing from historical trauma is connected to political action, such as reclaiming their land, taking back control of their own governments and social services, protesting environmental destruction and revitalizing their own ceremonies and traditions.

Maria Yellow Horse Brave Heart,
a Lakota scholar, first coined
the term historical trauma to
describe the emotional toll when
a whole community or nation
experiences many horrible things,
including displacement from
their land, deadly diseases,
starvation, murders and
dehumanizing laws.

Imagine how scary it is to live in a place where you can't even use the words that naturally roll off your tongue. Imagine if you said these words aloud and you got smacked in the head. How confusing and frightening this would be. Really, these places were more like prisons than schools.

These children were repeatedly told that their culture was evil and dirty. Taken from their communities, they were torn from their traditions and identity. Taken from their homes, many grew up without the love and affection that their families would have provided.

In addition to experiencing the trauma of residential schools, Indigenous Peoples across Turtle Island and throughout the world have had their lands stolen by settlers. And they have been severely impacted by a long history of racism.

When people have been traumatized, they look for ways to stop the pain and dull the memories. This often means coping in unhealthy ways and being unable to connect emotionally with others, even their own children. Trauma is then passed down from generation to generation. This is called intergenerational trauma.

I think of how my Mennonite grandparents came to this country from Ukraine. They had been subjected to violence and terror in their homeland, so trauma has been passed down in my family too. But when my ancestors built a new home in Canada, they were part of a wave of settlers displacing Indigenous people from their lands. The Canadian government was selling the land dirt cheap, and Indigenous people were being forced onto tiny reserves.

I know now that my comfortable life is a result of the living my family made on this stolen land and the privilege I have because I'm white. In contrast, many Indigenous communities now suffer from the highest rates of anxiety, depression, **substance abuse**, violence and suicide. This is an immense injustice.

"INDIGENOUS PEOPLES HAVE ALWAYS KEPT ALIVE THEIR OWN WAYS OF KNOWING AND BEING."

And yet Indigenous Peoples have always kept alive their own ways of knowing and being. Research has shown that in Indigenous communities where traditional cultural practices are thriving, the suicide rates are dramatically lower—and often even more so in communities that have control over their own land, government, health care and education. For many Indigenous people, the healing journey is both personal and political. It involves fixing historical injustices, and this is something we can all be part of.

INDIGENOUS TEACHINGS

*S*usan Landell was thirty when she went to her first sweat lodge ceremony. Sitting in the deep darkness, inhaling the tangy cedar, while the hot rocks glowed in the center and prayer and songs were lifted, Susan knew this was the beginning of her spiritual journey.

Susan Landell

Susan is Cree and Métis. She was born in Montreal and now lives on Vancouver Island, where she has been an art therapist for 25 years. Susan has two Elders who are her guides— David Sommerville and Leah Siebold, whose medicine names are Spirit Eagle and Many Shawls Woman. Susan's own medicine name is Evening Rainbow. "You have the potential of the name within you," she says, "and you grow into it." Evening Rainbow is fitting, as Susan uses lots of color in her art. And as a Métis person, she sees herself as a bridge between worlds.

Smudging is a sacred ceremony, practiced by many Indigenous Peoples, where plant medicine is burned and the smoke is used to purify the heart, mind, spirit and body.

Susan invites me to breathe in the scents of her sacred medicines: tobacco, sweetgrass, sage and cedar. She says that when you smudge, you gather the smoke like water to wash your body. She lights the sage, and as the smoke rises, our prayers rise too. This is a sacred ceremony that happens in silence. Susan says smudging with sage is cleansing and can help you cope with depression, grief, anxiety and all kinds of negative feelings.

"It's always bugged me that the spiritual is missing from mental health," Susan says. "We're missing the boat."

In Susan's work with youth, she likes to take them outside. Susan will ask the youth to pick a tree and lean against it and feel the energy of the tree. "What's the dream that's there?" she will ask. Or she asks them to stand in a stream and just focus on the feel of the water. Or she'll take them to the beach and have them build driftwood forts. "It's all there," she says. "Nature is inherently healing for everyone."

In mainstream, non-Indigenous North American culture, mental health tends to focus on the individual and the individual's mind.

While each Indigenous culture is distinct, most focus more on the interconnectedness of each person with family, with community and with the land. Across Turtle Island and around the world, Indigenous people are reclaiming their culture, ceremonies and lands, and in doing so, are nurturing their well-being.

MICHAEL HART IS a member of the Fisher River Cree Nation and is the Canada Research Chair in Indigenous Knowledges and Social Work. He teaches about mino-pimatisiwin, a Cree word that can be translated as "the good life" or "being alive well." More than just "mental health," mino-pimatisiwin captures the idea that a person's wellness includes good relationships with family, community and the earth. It's about balancing the mind, body, emotions and spirit.

Michael Hart

This is illustrated in the medicine wheel, which shows how each aspect of being is part of the whole and can't be thought of in isolation. In the Cree worldview, the source of distress is an imbalance in the unity of being. Finding mino-pimatisiwin is a lifelong process of seeking balance and wholeness, both within oneself and in all one's relations.

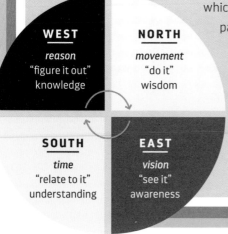

WEST
reason
"figure it out"
knowledge

NORTH
movement
"do it"
wisdom

SOUTH
time
"relate to it"
understanding

EAST
vision
"see it"
awareness

Jack Linklater Jr.

ON CONNECTING WITH NATURE

" **HELLO, MY NAME IS JACK LINKLATER JR.** I live in Attawapiskat, Ontario. I am Cree and proud to be. I live along the James Bay shorelines, the lowlands of the Mushkegowuk territory. My message to you if you're having a hard time: Look to the tree, as it shows you to stand tall and proud. Look to the rock, as it shows you the strength you need. Look to the river, as it shows you to keep moving forward in life, as it flows, and to never give up. To the flowers, as it shows you the love you need, the colors. The grass, as it teaches you forgiveness, as it always grows and grows no matter if you keep stepping on it. It's there to show you to forgive. We matter. Every living thing matters. The trees, the rocks, the flowers. You matter. Stay strong."

2

SINNERS, BEASTS OR FOOLS?

THE AWFUL HISTORY OF "TREATING" MENTAL ILLNESS AND THE EFFORTS FOR REFORM

FROM ANCIENT TIMES to the present day, mental illness has been viewed as a perplexing, ominous and darkly fascinating phenomenon. Society's treatment of people who have been labeled *insane* or *lunatic* has caused great suffering and tragedy. Mental illness has been used to justify torture and imprisonment. As the causes of distress have been debated, so have the treatments. Let's take a look at the historical evolution of our understanding.

The Extraction of the Stone of Madness, *a painting made around 1494 by Hieronymus Bosch, depicts trepanation. In the book* Madness and Civilization, *Michel Foucault says,* "Bosch's famous doctor is far more insane than the patient he is attempting to cure."

POSSESSED BY SPIRITS

Throughout the ages, descriptions of bizarre behavior pepper stories from every culture. In many ancient societies, when someone was hallucinating or acting oddly it was thought that they were possessed by a good or evil spirit. A person possessed by a good spirit was treated with awe and respect, as someone with special powers or mystical messages from the gods. An evil spirit meant the person was being punished by the gods and needed to be "cured."

In Christian traditions, casting out an evil spirit often involved prayers and chanting. In Hinduism, exorcism included burning incense and sprinkling water from holy rivers. In Islamic traditions, it involved special perfumes called ittars. In Judaism, the rabbi might blow a ram's horn to shake loose the spirit from the person's body. What all these traditions have in common is a ritual in which a person with spiritual authority calls on a higher power to evict the evil spirit.

Even before written records, archaeological evidence shows that a surgical procedure called trepanation was performed as long as 8,500 years ago. This may have been the earliest treatment for mental disorders. A shaman or spiritual leader would use a stone tool to chip a hole into the person's skull so the evil spirit could escape.

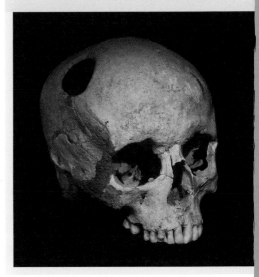

This Neolithic skull shows a trepanation hole. This person likely survived the "treatment" because the edges of the hole are rounded with new bone growth.

NATURAL CAUSES
GREEK MEDICINE

During the Golden Age of Greece (500–300 BCE), Hippocrates was renowned as a doctor who dedicated himself to carefully observing his patients and documenting their symptoms. Hippocrates rejected the idea that diseases were punishments sent from a deity. Instead, he believed diseases had natural causes. This radical idea established medicine as a field of study separate from religion.

Hippocrates's case studies showed that a person's health was affected by things like climate, food, water and living conditions.

He noted that blows to the head could change a person's ability to walk, speak and think. These observations helped to create the understanding that the brain controlled human perceptions and behaviors, and that the brain, like any other organ, could be affected by disease.

Hippocrates

At this time, human bodies had not yet been dissected and studied. So the Greeks knew almost nothing about the internal workings of the body. Hippocrates believed there were four essential substances running through our bodies: black bile, yellow bile, phlegm and blood. He thought each person had a unique mixture of these substances, called "the four humors," and that this determined their personality.

While we now know this theory to be inaccurate, a belief in the link between the body, personality and behavior drove further investigation into the causes of psychological distress.

From 1891 to 1893 Edvard Munch painted multiple versions of this scene entitled Melancholy.

EARLY ISLAMIC MEDICINE AND BIMARISTANS

Despite the theories of the early Greeks, during the Middle Ages (about 500–1500 CE), the common belief in European countries was that unusual behavior was caused by supernatural phenomena. There was little scientific investigation, and the understanding of mental disorders stalled. Treatment mostly involved prayer and exorcism or locking people away.

In the early Islamic world, things were very different. Islamic medicine preserved many aspects of the Greek scientific knowledge and investigated further. As early as 707 CE, Islamic societies built **bimaristans**, hospitals with special wards for people with mental diseases, and the first to be staffed by physicians who were paid salaries and had to pass special licensing exams to practice. These physicians approached medicine in a secular, scientific manner, with careful observation and documentation of patients' symptoms to better understand the causes of disease.

As much as possible, patients were allowed to move about freely. They were well fed and families were often involved in their daily care. Bimaristans were built in beautiful locations. It was believed that fresh air, gardens and even a river running through the court-yard would create a therapeutic environment. The scents of flowers and herbs were used as calming remedies, as were the soothing gurgles of fountains. Live music and theater were used to improve patients' moods. What a completely different atmosphere from that of the asylums and hospitals of the Western world. Early Islamic societies offered a much more advanced and humane approach than anywhere else in the world would for hundreds of years.

AVICENNA (980–1037 CE)
was known as the "prince of physicians" in the Islamic world by the time he was 18 years old. He went on to write a massive book called *The Canon of Medicine* that would be the go-to medical text in medieval Europe and the Islamic world for the next 700 years.

Seven centuries before doctors in European countries, Avicenna thought diseases had natural causes. He developed the idea that the mind influences the body in subtle ways. For example, he wrote about how if you are creeping along a narrow plank suspended over a deep chasm and your mind pictures you tumbling into the raging river below, you will likely fall. This sounds a lot like the sports psychology of today, where athletes, and the scientists who study athletic feats, know that visualizing a good performance can help make it happen.

ASYLUMS AND HOSPITALS

The word *asylum* means a place of sanctuary, but in the mental health realm it conjures up images of dank cells and chains. While asylums started as church-run places of refuge for those who had no place to live, they gradually became more like prisons. From the 16th century on, asylums grew more and more crowded as anyone who didn't fit into society was locked up.

The Bethlem Royal Hospital, which opened in 1247 in London, was one of the very first insane asylums. It gained such a reputation for chaos that its nickname— Bedlam—became a word meaning "a scene of uproar and confusion."

Many of the patients were locked in solitary confinement. The sewer regularly backed up. Food was scarce. By the 17th

This etching depicts James Norris, an American marine, who was chained in this position for 12 years in the "incurable" ward at Bethlem.

century, Bethlem had medical staff and had become known as a hospital for the insane. However, the "treatments" were extremely harsh. It was believed that inducing vomiting, purging the bowels, and bloodletting could rid the body of madness.

In one treatment, called "rotational therapy," the patient was placed in a chair suspended from the ceiling and spun as fast as possible until they vomited. Patients were often dunked in ice baths. We now know that many people were buried in mass graves at the site.

For many years, Bethlem made money by charging the public to come and gawk at the troubled, helpless patients. Some thought that allowing the public to visit would teach a frightening lesson about the dangers of immorality. Or that it would inspire compassion and charity. But mostly it was entertainment, a spectacle of misery that thrilled curious onlookers.

While Bethlem has inspired horror films, the early asylums in the United States and Canada were no better. A common philosophy of treatment was that patients could be scared or intimidated into rationality. The patients were often still seen as simply sinners, beasts or fools.

HYSTERIA

YOU'VE PROBABLY HEARD the word *hysterical* used to describe someone having an emotional meltdown. It's often used as a put-down to imply that their reaction is irrational and over the top.

The word *hysteria* comes from the Greek word *hystera*, which means uterus. In ancient Greece, some thought the uterus was like a wandering animal that moved about a woman's body and put pressure on other organs, causing nervousness, difficulty breathing, fainting and irritability. For centuries, it was thought that if women were not married or not having "proper" sex with their husbands, they would be prone to hysteria.

This contributed to the idea that women are physically and emotionally inferior to men. Feminists argue that hysteria was used as just another way to discredit women's emotions and blame women for valid reactions to living in conditions that were sexist and harmful.

MELANCHOLIA

ACCORDING TO HIPPOCRATES, melancholia was caused by excessive amounts of "black bile," a cold, muddy sediment that produced "fears and despondencies." Hildegard of Bingen (1098–1179), the first woman physician to publish a medical text, thought of melancholia as a defect of the soul caused by sin.

By the 16th and 17th centuries, being moody and brooding was thought to be a mark of artistic genius in the European art and literary scenes. Jump to the 1980s and '90s, when emo bands created angsty music that explored alienation, self-hatred and even *suicidal thoughts*. Emo and other art forms have been called out for glamorizing depression, which is actually a painful and debilitating condition. Yet through art and music the most difficult human emotions can be shared. Finding a song or poem that just perfectly captures your feelings can be a huge comfort.

Today, the World Health Organization says that more than 300 million people worldwide are affected by depression and that it is the leading cause of disability.

This painting by Tony Robert-Fleury depicts Dr. Philippe Pinel finally removing the chains from the patients at the Hospice de la Salpêtrière in Paris.

HUMANITARIAN REFORM

ooking back, it's hard to imagine how such cruel treatment was justified. Cultural ideas can be so pervasive that they're taken for granted as "just the way it is." It often takes radical thinkers to explore out-of-the-box ideas and start championing new ways of doing things. Here are the stories of a few key people who were passionate advocates for humanitarian mental health reform.

PHILIPPE PINEL AND MORAL TREATMENT

Philippe Pinel (1745–1826), a young French physician, had a friend who slid into depression. When his friend took his own life, Pinel was shocked that more hadn't been done to help him. Pinel decided he wanted to understand the workings of the human mind in order to help people and save lives.

Eventually, Pinel got a job at Bicêtre Hospital, where 4,000 men were imprisoned, 200 of them considered insane. That's where he met Jean-Baptiste Pussin (1745–1811), the head of the mental ward. Pussin wasn't a doctor, but Pinel saw his skill in relating to each patient as a unique individual. Pinel realized he had to stop acting like the expert and start listening.

Pinel took the time to hear each patient's story. He met with patients daily, took detailed notes and began compiling hundreds of case studies. These studies were sympathetic and respectful. No one had written like this about patients before. In vivid detail he described the struggles of a clockmaker who was obsessed with perpetual motion, an engineer who wore himself out at work and an elderly man who identified as a young woman and loved to chat about clothes and hopes for marriage.

Pinel noticed that his patients came from all walks of life, but what they had in common was that they each felt like aliens in the regular world. That's why doctors who worked with the mentally ill were called alienists before the word *psychiatrist* came into being.

Pinel marveled at the sensitivity of his patients. He saw that people who had the capacity for compassion and introspection could be vulnerable to life's ups and downs. Pinel also recognized that

Animal therapy is becoming increasingly popular as science shows that the Quakers were on to something—hanging out with an animal improves mental health. Grooming a horse or petting a dog reduces loneliness, anxiety and depression. One study showed that even petting a turtle relieves stress, but only if it's a living turtle and not a toy. Another study showed that seniors who each cared for five crickets became less depressed in as little as eight weeks. Simply caring for another living being, whether cuddly or not, may be good medicine.

difficult experiences, such as heartbreak, failure, religious disillusionment, financial ruin or unsatisfied ambition, could unhinge a person's grasp on reason.

Pinel believed that the doctor had to be able to travel into the alien world of the patient to understand their perspective and lead them back to "sanity". He also realized that if patients were treated with basic respect, they often recovered on their own.

Pinel's approach became known as "traitement moral," or moral treatment. *Moral* in this case didn't refer to right and wrong so much as to a more psychological approach that focused on the emotional well-being of patients. While this approach still sometimes used intimidation and straitjackets, it was a big improvement over keeping people in chains for years on end. Pinel firmly believed that kindness, hope and time were the best cures.

THE YORK RETREAT

At the same time as Pinel was reforming treatment in France, the Quakers, a religious group in England, were developing a treatment based on their values of nonviolence and equality.

The York Retreat was a small farm where the residents could work and enjoy the peaceful natural surroundings.

Hannah Mills, a young Quaker widow, had been admitted to York Asylum for melancholy. Six weeks later she was found dead. Suspecting extreme mistreatment, the local Quaker community was shocked and saddened. William Tuke (1732–1822), a prominent Quaker and a businessman, decided to buy a parcel of land and build a farm where mentally disturbed people could live. His vision was to create a place where kindness and acceptance would help people to recover.

The staff and patients at the York Retreat were called family. Quakers believed that the light of God lived within each person and that nothing, not even madness, could snuff it out.

The York Retreat residents ate healthy food and were encouraged to read, write, make crafts and pray. Chains and physical punishment were not allowed. Fear and boredom, it was believed, could make people worse. So the residents worked outside and took care of animals. The Quakers believed that affectionate, respectful relationships with animals and other humans could inspire self-esteem and self-control in patients. While this approach had a distinctly religious foundation, it influenced psychiatric care around the world.

Dorothea Dix

DOROTHEA DIX AND REFORM IN AMERICA

In America, Dorothea Dix (1802–1887) was a fierce advocate for mental health reform. Dix grew up in a troubled home, with a mother who suffered from depression and a father who drank too much and had a harsh, unpredictable bent. She had a lonely, difficult childhood and often skipped school in her teenage years.

As an adult, Dix struggled with periods of depression. To rest and recover, she took a vacation to Europe, where she was inspired by the peaceful York Retreat and by the idea that the government should play an active role in taking care of its most vulnerable citizens.

When Dix took a job teaching at a prison in East Cambridge, Massachusetts, she was shocked by the dirty, inhumane conditions. People who were mentally ill were imprisoned alongside violent criminals. The guards doled out insults and

Mental Health America made this bell out of the shackles and chains that had bound mental health patients. The inscription reads, "Cast from shackles which bound them, this bell shall ring out hope for the mentally ill and victory over mental illness."

cruelty. So Dix hit the road and traveled all over Massachusetts to investigate how mentally ill people were treated.

She used vivid descriptions of the neglect and abuse to move political leaders to action. In an era when women couldn't vote or hold political positions, she wrote "memorials" that were read out by a man in the legislature. She refused to soften her language and laid bare the facts, describing people languishing "in cages, closets, cellars, stalls, pens! Chained, naked, beaten with rods and lashed into obedience!"

As a result of her relentless advocacy, more than 30 hospitals for the treatment of the mentally ill were established in the United States and Canada.

3

MODERN CURES?

PSYCHOTHERAPY, PSYCHIATRY AND COMMUNITY TREATMENT

BY THE END of the 19th century, public asylums had grown dramatically in size and were generally overcrowded and run-down. The ideals of moral treatment had mostly been forgotten or pushed aside. Seventy years after Pinel had first taken the chains off his patients, asylums were once again simply warehouses for the sick, doing nothing more than confining them and keeping them out of sight. Often it wasn't even believed that people could recover from mental illness. But new developments came rushing in with the 20th century.

With the rise of modern science came the idea that the brain could be understood as a machine. If we could just figure out how it worked, we could fix it.

Microscopes and brain dissections helped neuroscientists under-stand that certain regions of the brain controlled certain functions. This became clear when looking at the brains of people who had suffered head injuries. However, when it came to mental illness, microscopes could not pick up any differences between a healthy brain and a brain from a person with mental illness. Understand-ing the biology of mental illness would have to wait for advances in neurochemistry.

THE TALKING CURE

A t the beginning of the 20th century, a German medical doctor named Sigmund Freud (1856–1939) turned away from medi-cine and began thinking about how mental disturbances might be caused by repressed or forgotten childhood experiences.

Freud is renowned for having developed **psychoanalysis**, the "talking cure" in which patients are encouraged to talk freely about whatever memories, dreams or ideas come to mind. Freud believed that in addition to our conscious, easily accessible thoughts, we each have a deep well of impulses, drives and memories that are harder to understand and control. The goal of therapy was to bring these hidden thoughts into consciousness to free the patient from emotional pain.

Psychoanalysis was a major part of psychiatry during the first half of the 20th century. However, many critics say Freud's theories have always been just elaborate guesses at the workings of the mind, and not testable scientific theories. Feminists have critiqued Freud's view of women as demeaning and inaccurate. And many of his views on sexuality now seem outdated and outlandish.

Once psychiatric medications arrived on the scene, psychiatry became much more focused on treating severe mental illness with

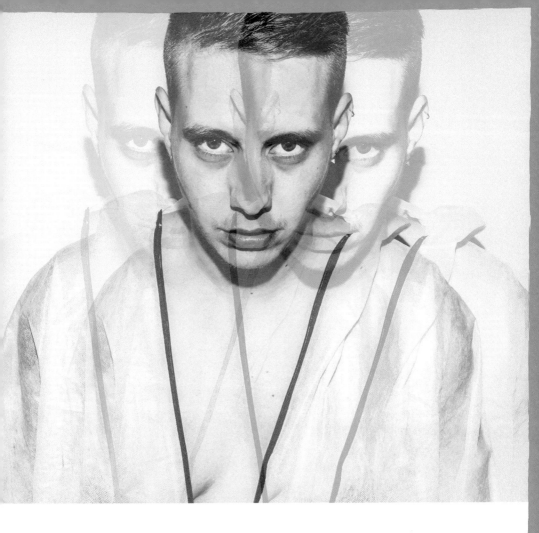

medications, often leaving talk therapy up to other professions such as psychologists, social workers and counselors. Many brilliant therapists, such as Carl Jung, Alfred Adler, B.F. Skinner and Carl Rogers, developed theories of why people experience emotional difficulties and how to work with feelings, thoughts and behaviors to find wellness. Today there are over 350 forms of counseling and **psychotherapy**. While talk therapy has branched into many different schools of thought, many of Freud's ideas are still influential, including the most basic one—that talking about your problems can be helpful.

THE PROMISE OF PSYCHIATRIC MEDICATIONS

long with a focus on the brain, the 20th century brought a surge of new experimental physical therapies, such as malario-therapy, insulin coma therapy and electroconvulsive therapy (shock therapy). One of the most drastic interventions, lobotomy, involved a surgical procedure to separate the frontal lobes from the rest of the brain. While lobotomies were intended to reduce distressing symptoms, many patients were left intellectually impaired and emotionally blunted. Some died on the operating table or later by suicide.

In contrast to these invasive procedures, the promise of psychiatric medications created great hope. When the first antipsychotic medication, chlorpromazine, was tested with psychiatric patients, the results were profound. Many delirious patients came out of their confusion, many psychotic patients stopped hearing voices and some depressed patients revived. By 1955, psychiatrists all over North America who had never used medications before were prescribing chlorpromazine and seeing promising results.

But no one understood exactly how the drug worked. Many theories about how antipsychotic drugs work have been put forward in the last 60 years, but none have yet been proved.

It wasn't until 1987 that Prozac hit the market. In just a few years, over two million people were taking this anti-depressant to boost their mood. Now there are many drugs similar to Prozac, yet only about a third of patients find that these medications relieve their symptoms. Even though there have been many studies, it's unclear why some people get better with medications and others don't.

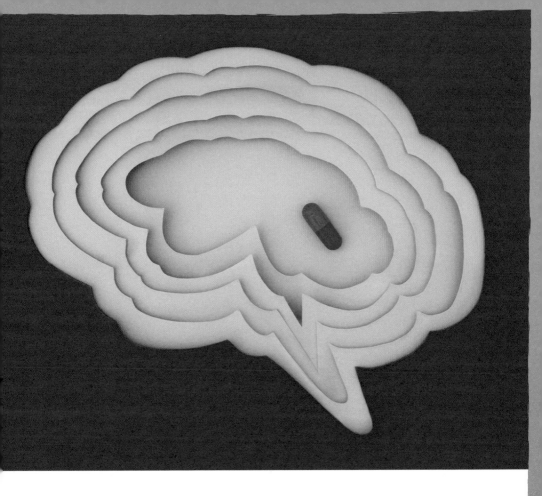

To doctors and patients alike, the idea of a quick fix can be appealing. Getting a prescription is often a lot easier than accessing ongoing support and counseling. But it's not a sure fix, and there are often side effects. Many critics warn that pharmaceutical companies are making fat profits on psychiatric medications. Research suggests that things like exercise, meditation, yoga and different forms of counseling can often be just as effective as medications, if not more so. That said, medications can provide relief from debilitating symptoms and medications can help some people have enough energy, motivation and calmness so they can make it to appointments and engage in healthy activities, kickstarting wellness.

PSYCHIATRY'S BIBLE: THE DSM

n medicine, being able to accurately diagnose diseases is the hallmark of professional credibility. In 1952, the publication of the *Diagnostic and Statistical Manual of Mental Disorders*—often called the *DSM*—marked the American Psychiatric Association's push for psychiatry to be taken seriously as a medical specialty. The current version, DSM-5, lays out 22 categories of disorders, including anxiety, mood, trauma, sex, gender, substance use and psychotic disorders. Under these broad categories, it sets out the specific criteria for hundreds of psychiatric disorders.

This classification system is based on observable patterns of symptoms, not on actual biological markers of disease. This is why the DSM uses the word *disorder* rather than *disease*.

Critics of psychiatry point out that what is considered normal and abnormal is strongly influenced by culture. While there is a technical definition of normal, which is about statistical averages, the word *normal* often gets loaded with judgments about what is good versus bad, or socially acceptable versus unacceptable. For example, when the DSM was first published, homosexuality was listed as a disorder. It was considered abnormal and therefore defective. After much controversy, it was removed in 1973 when the American Psychiatric Association finally declared that "homosexuality per se implies no impairment in judgment, stability, reliability, or general social or vocational capabilities."

Since our society gives privilege and power to people who are closer to what is considered "normal," being labeled as having a "disorder" can be a real disadvantage. Not to mention that it can affect your sense of yourself. Another problem is that people

"THE WORD NORMAL OFTEN GETS LOADED WITH JUDGMENTS ABOUT WHAT IS GOOD VERSUS BAD, OR SOCIALLY ACCEPTABLE VERSUS UNACCEPTABLE."

who are already more marginalized in society are more likely to be diagnosed with a mental disorder. The DSM has been criticized as an inadequate tool, one that can be misleading because it promotes a false sense of certainty about diagnoses. However, diagnoses can also be useful in understanding the nature and severity of a person's symptoms and prescribing treatments known to be helpful.

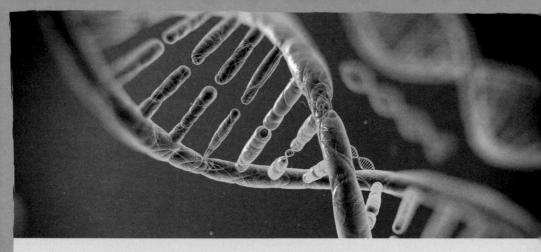

The Psychiatric Genomics Consortium is a group of over 800 researchers from all over the world who are investigating the genomes of nearly one million people. These large sample sizes are helping scientists understand the complex genetic variations that may make some people more susceptible to mental illness.

GENETIC RESEARCH

While the underlying biological causes of mental illness have remained elusive, psychiatric genetics is currently attempting to decode the mysteries by looking at DNA.

Genetic research opens a window into the most basic building blocks of our human bodies: our genes. These are the instructions that get passed down from parents to children and tell our cells how to build a body that works. Genes determine things like eye color, skin color and height—and really every facet of our physical existence.

With the discovery that certain diseases, like cystic fibrosis, are caused by single gene abnormalities, there was hope for a breakthrough in identifying the causes of psychiatric disorders. However, it was soon discovered that psychiatric disorders are caused by the interplay of many gene variations plus environmental factors like the food we eat, the chemicals we're exposed to or even the stress in our lives.

There are likely hundreds or even thousands of genetic variations at play. Many are yet to be discovered. Harvard researcher

Jordan Smoller has said that figuring out the genetic causes of mental illness is like trying to write down the music for a symphony when you can only hear a handful of the notes.

Genetic researchers have confirmed the long-held suspicion that many psychiatric disorders run in families, often with more than one disorder clustering together. For example, depression and anxiety tend to occur together in families. So do **mood disorders**, **attention deficit hyperactivity disorder (ADHD)** and substance abuse. This kind of overlap gives us a clue that what we now consider to be distinct diagnoses, according to the DSM, might actually have a common biological basis.

Genetic research also points toward the idea that there is no sharp boundary between "normal" and "disordered." For example, one study showed that the same genetic factors that show up in children diagnosed with ADHD also show up in children who have milder symptoms of inattention and hyperactivity. There's no simple on or off switch for a given disorder.

A big question remains: will genetic research lead to new diagnoses based on "hard" science? It might not be quick or easy, but further research could lead the evolution in how we understand and treat mental disorders.

QUESTIONING PSYCHIATRY

Many questions have dogged psychiatry. Has psychiatry led to compassionate, effective treatments or has it labeled and stigmatized human suffering? Does it treat legitimate diseases or does it mostly target people who are already marginalized? Is it helping people or controlling people?

Psychiatry has promoted some of the most controversial practices in modern medicine, such as the use of solitary confinement, physical

Supported by many prominent psychiatrists in the early 20th century, eugenics was a powerful social movement based on the flawed and racist idea that the society could be "improved" by preventing people judged as "unfit" from having children. As this photo of an exhibit at a Kansas state fair shows, for a time these ideas were widely accepted by the public in the United States, as well as in Canada and many European countries. Eventually, these ideas contributed to the mass exterminations of the Nazi Holocaust in Germany.

and chemical restraints (drugs used to sedate patients), electro-convulsive therapy, lobotomies and eugenics (selective breeding and forced sterilization).

Many people who have experienced poor psychiatric treatment have risen up in protest, creating a grassroots psychiatric survivor movement. Survivors and their allies have many different viewpoints. Some protest certain practices that seem the most barbaric. Others want patients and their families to have more say in what sort of services are available and to be treated with respect. Still others take an anti-psychiatry approach, declaring that the science is bogus, that diagnoses are phony labels made up by powerful white men to oppress the vulnerable, and that the whole system is driven by the desire for profit and power.

MAD PRIDE

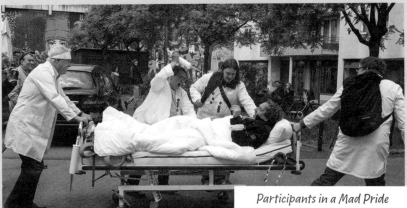

Participants in a Mad Pride parade in Cologne, Germany.

THE MAD PRIDE MOVEMENT was born out of people's frustrations with mental health services that they experienced as unhelpful and demeaning. Some people have reclaimed the word *mad* as an identity to be proud of. These activists question the idea that being "normal" is a good thing. Maybe *normal* is another word for being shut down, boring and oppressed, they say. Maybe madness is something to be celebrated, not controlled. Or maybe it's the world that is mad—with its inequality, greed and violence—and that's what makes people unwell. Mad Pride advocates for the freedom of all people to express themselves in creative and unconventional ways without being shamed, locked up or drugged up for it. This isn't to say that people don't suffer, just that suffering shouldn't be labeled as disordered or bad. There are also many mental health activists who don't identify as "mad" but, based on their lived experiences, advocate for more compassionate, ethical and effective treatment.

CULTURE, RACE AND POWER

During the 19th and 20th centuries, the dominant medical opinion assumed that "primitive" peoples were less affected by mental illness than people of European descent. *Primitive* is a loaded word used to imply that a culture is less developed. It has historically been used by white people to refer to people of African descent and Indigenous Peoples the world over. For a long time, white cultures promoted the idea that madness was a breakdown of reasoning and moral judgment, and that these "higher faculties" of reason weren't as developed in "uncivilized" peoples. This was clearly an incorrect and racist idea.

Chester Pierce (1927–2016) was an African American psychiatrist who founded Black Psychiatrists of America. He spent his career challenging his colleagues to consider how race and racism affect mental health.

Some medical experts put forward the idea that "dark-skinned peoples" had less-developed nervous systems, so when they were exposed to the stresses of civilization, they were more vulnerable to insanity. Proslavery supporters even argued that slavery was good for Black people because it meant their needs were taken care of, whereas freed Black people were more likely to go insane.

Today, most psychiatrists are trained to be aware of their own cultural assumptions and to consider the role of culture in any interaction. Culture shapes how we see ourselves and the world. It also plays a role in how people experience distress and make meaning out of it.

THE LAFARGUE CLINIC
IN HARLEM

IN 1946, THE LAFARGUE MENTAL HYGIENE CLINIC opened in Harlem, New York. It was run out of a church in this mostly Black neighborhood and offered therapy to local residents regardless of their skin color or ability to pay.

The staff, from various racial and professional backgrounds, identified as "universalists" and believed there were no innate psychological differences between people of different skin color or race. Instead of framing Black psyches as inferior or defective, the clinic blamed white supremacy (the belief that white people are better than other races) as the true problem. They worked from a recognition that racism and poverty create extreme psychological stress. The Lafargue Clinic helped clients think of their problems in terms of social inequality and discrimination rather than as personal failings.

The Lafargue Clinic staff provided mental health services but also knew the Harlem community and helped people deal with practical problems like unemployment, poverty and housing.

Power difference can also come into play. For many people who have experienced discrimination, just being in a hospital or clinic can create a lot of anxiety. The patient and the **mental health professionals** often have very different social statuses. People who are professionals have usually had a lot of advantages—like money, a safe home, healthy food, a good education—throughout their life and may have trouble relating to people who have grown up with the odds stacked against them. Professionals hold a lot of power, as they are considered experts and can make decisions that will affect patients' futures. Meanwhile patients are in a place of feeling unwell and may be quite vulnerable. The quality of care a patient receives is impacted if the patient doesn't feel comfortable opening up or if the professional is relying on stereotypes and assumptions.

To be effective and respectful, people who provide mental health services must consider cultural difference to be an important piece of the puzzle and work to make it culturally safe for people to access care.

DEINSTITUTIONALIZATION

FROM CONFINEMENT TO THE COMMUNITY

long with the development of psychiatric medications, the 1950s and 1960s brought another push for mental health reform. It was hoped that people who were mentally ill could move out of institutions and live more healthy, ordinary lives in the community.

Advocates for deinstitutionalization pointed out that psychiatric hospitals were overcrowded and run-down. They were dull and overly strict places, if not downright depressing and frightening. Advocates believed that long stays in these institutions were actually making people more helpless and dependent instead of better.

With deinstitutionalization, many people who had lived most of their lives in psychiatric hospitals were moved into the community—some to their own apartments, some to group homes and many back to their families. Many psychiatric hospitals were closed altogether, replaced by smaller psychiatric wards in general hospitals. The goal was to admit fewer people to hospital and, when people were admitted, to make sure their hospital stay was as short as possible.

Psychiatric hospitals were incredibly expensive to operate, so closing beds meant big savings for governments. While there are many positive aspects to community-based care, the shift wasn't supported with adequate funding for community services, and many people haven't gotten the care they need.

IN THE UNITED STATES in the mid-1950s, there were around 640,000 patients in psychiatric hospitals. By the 1980s, there were fewer than 100,000. In Canada over roughly the same 30-year period, the number of psychiatric beds was reduced by over 70 percent, followed by further cuts in the following decades. Without proper care, many people with mental health problems have become homeless.

Families have been left to do much of the caregiving work, assuming the roles of counselor, case manager, advocate and mobile crisis unit, while also providing housing, financial support, food and social connection for their loved ones.

Many people who don't have families to pick up the slack have become homeless. Many others have ended up in prisons, criminalized for being poor and mentally ill and simply trying to survive.

Access to housing that is safe, comfortable and stable is one of the biggest factors in mental and physical well-being. While housing is

ACCORDING TO THE National Alliance on Mental Illness, 15 percent of men and 30 percent of women in American prisons are living with a serious mental illness that often goes undiagnosed and untreated. Additionally, many youth and adults who are imprisoned have had traumatic childhood experiences. More and more, crisis intervention teams and jail diversion programs are trying to help people get treatment instead of jail time.

often very difficult to find for people who struggle with serious mental illness, there are some publicly funded residential care facilities that provide a safe place to live with staff support. When I worked in a residential treatment program, I liked working the holidays. I'd come in early in the morning on Christmas or Thanksgiving and put the turkey in the oven. A few of the residents would help peel the potatoes, decorate the table and select the tunes to make it feel like a celebration.

Many of the residents experienced intense hallucinations and delusions. And many of them had experienced abuse, often in childhood. Some of them seemed almost vacant of emotion or motivation. Some had difficulty with basic tasks such as laundry, showering and keeping house. Everyone was on an extremely limited budget of government money, meaning they could barely afford food and were often stressed about money. Many had no family or friends who visited. So these celebrations were important.

The residents had diagnoses like schizophrenia and **bipolar disorder.** Like clockwork, I would hand out medications—morning meds, noon meds, dinner meds, evening meds. Some people had a

"ACCESS TO HOUSING THAT IS SAFE, COMFORTABLE AND STABLE IS ONE OF THE BIGGEST FACTORS IN MENTAL AND PHYSICAL WELL-BEING."

A home is more than just a place to sleep—it is an essential part of building a calm nervous system, healthy routines and a sense of dignity and belonging. Research has shown that a "housing first" approach—where people are given a home along with mental health support—is effective in improving people's wellness and can actually save society the money that would otherwise be spent on emergency services.

big handful of meds to swallow, all with me watching carefully to make sure that they didn't "cheek" them.

Most of the residents were on "involuntary status." This meant they were on doctor's orders to take their medications and maintain a stable place of residence. Some didn't want to take medications, but they were forced to. If they didn't, we could call the police, who would find them and take them to the hospital for evaluation and possibly keep them on a locked ward against their will.

If it weren't for this program, most of these people likely would have been living on the streets. And yet, in exchange for a home, they were subjected to things like apartment inspections, curfews and rules that most adults don't have to deal with, not to mention being forced to take meds. It can be a complicated trade-off. And yet it gave me some comfort to make a nice meal and share a few laughs and some holiday spirit.

POLICING ON THE FRONT LINES OF MENTAL HEALTH

*W*ith *deinstitutionalization and* inadequate funding for mental health services, people have trouble finding the help they need. They often get worse and worse until they are in major crisis. And this is when the police are called in. Increasingly, the police have had to become frontline mental health workers.

I remember getting in my car and hearing on the radio that a twenty-year-old man named Rhett had been shot by police in my neighborhood. He had been threatening suicide, so his mom called 9-1-1. She says that when the police arrived, he was sitting calmly on the couch. Minutes later, he was dead.

Rhett began having troubles as a young boy but never got the mental health help he needed. His mom had called the police before for help dealing with her son's aggressive behavior, and it had always ended peacefully. But this time things went sideways.

A neighbor says that through the thin walls of the duplex he heard police yelling at Rhett. With a steak knife in hand, Rhett ran at the police. Then he was shot.

At the inquest, all four police officers involved in the situation that ended Rhett's life broke down and cried on the stand. They were cleared of any wrongdoing. And yet this death still feels like a terrible, unnecessary tragedy.

I think of all the times I've had to call the police because one of my clients or someone I love was in a mental health crisis—sending messages about ending it all or dancing carelessly in traffic or acting paranoid and erratic, getting worse and worse but refusing to go to the hospital. Every time, I've had a knot of fear in the pit of my stomach. It's a hard decision. On the one hand, I need help. On the other hand, I'm afraid that involving the police will escalate things. I worry that the person will be angry with me. Worst case, I worry that an encounter with the police will be scary and traumatizing or, even worse, things will escalate and someone will get hurt. I think of all the names in the news, all the struggling people who've ended up dead.

And yet, the police so often play an essential, difficult role. They are the only ones capable of conducting a missing persons search, breaking into someone's home, talking someone down or taking someone to the hospital against their will. Still, I imagine all the ways it could go so wrong. How scary is it for someone in extreme distress to face the uniforms, the guns—especially someone who has previously been abused by authority figures? How scary is it for the officers going in thinking someone is unstable, unpredictable and possibly armed?

Research has shown that police officers who have some training in mental health issues are more likely to use verbal negotiation rather than physical force. They are also more likely to connect the person in crisis with mental health resources rather than arresting them.

In Toronto, protestors draw attention to the killing of Sammy Yatim by police. A CBC documentary suggested that 40 percent of people killed by police in Canada were having a mental health crisis at the time they were shot. A report in the Washington Post estimated that in the United States at least 25 percent of the people killed by police have a serious mental illness.

De-escalation techniques aim to decrease the level of conflict in a situation. When police officers take the time to listen and give a person more space, they can develop more of a rapport. Remaining calm, moving slowly and talking in a calm voice in a tense situation can result in the person getting the help they need.

Many reports and advocacy groups have called for better training for police and more resources. Some cities now have mental health police units or officers dedicated to working on mobile crisis teams alongside nurses, counselors and social workers. There's good progress, but this is still a big area that our society needs to get better at.

ART'S STORY

For years, Constable Art Wlodyka worked on an emergency response team because he was attracted to the excitement of big, tactical responses to the most dangerous situations. Think busting through blockades, close-quarter combat, rescuing hostages.

Today he has a counseling degree and is credited as the driving force behind the creation of a mental health unit for the police department in New Westminster, British Columbia. Most days he wears a bulletproof vest over top of a polo shirt, and a plain jacket with cargo pants. It's a bit more casual than the standard uniform, but he's still armed with a gun. Yet, he says, it's the skill of listening that is his most important tool.

Art has been recognized by the Centre for Addiction and Mental Health as one of 150 Canadians who made a major contribution to the improvement of mental health services. Art says he grew up pretty sheltered. In his 20s, while working in Vancouver's city jail, he started listening to people's stories. He was amazed at what people had lived through.

"I realized there was no 'us' and 'them,'" he says now. He understood that people were not inherently bad. Rather, the people who ended up in jail were often victims of things they had no control over. Or they had faced struggles that many of us face, but they didn't have the safety nets to catch them on the way down.

Recently, Art met a man who had called the police over 150 times. Each time he'd say that people were stealing things from his apartment or implanting devices in his brain. Police would show up and figure

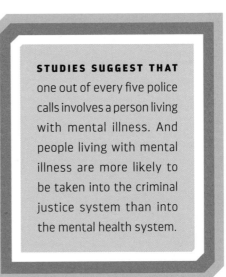

STUDIES SUGGEST THAT one out of every five police calls involves a person living with mental illness. And people living with mental illness are more likely to be taken into the criminal justice system than into the mental health system.

Constable Art Wlodyka

out that he was hearing or seeing things not based in reality. Eventually, they'd just listen to him for 30 seconds, tell him there was nothing they could do and leave. They were frustrated that he kept calling with "crazy" complaints.

Art remembers that even he was impatient. He'd call the man's mental health worker and insist that the man get a med change. But then Art got to thinking, what if I just listened to him? So he brought the man into a police interview room and sat down with him for an hour.

"It was a huge eye-opener," Art tells me. "This gentleman believed these things were happening and he just wanted to know that somebody cared about what he was experiencing." Having people not listen to him aggravated his paranoia, whereas having someone empathize with him soothed him. Not that it fixes everything. But being listened to is a very basic human need—something we all long for.

Art knows it's not always that easy. He's attended more than his share of overdoses and suicides. He's often involved in taking people to the hospital against their wishes. It's a tough job.

The shortage of mental health services means the police carry an extra-heavy burden of caring for people in distress. Yet in the police force, Art sees a shift toward greater understanding of mental health. He sees force and control being replaced by listening, patience and compassion.

"Art sees a shift toward greater understanding of mental health. He sees force and control being replaced by listening, patience and compassion."

Art's voice mail is full every day. He spends most of his time interacting with people who have severe and persistent mental illness. Many of these people are so ill that they have lost relationships with their families and friends. So Art is a lifeline for them.

Recently, Art attended a string of calls that each ended with a person being transported involuntarily to the hospital. Art says, "I felt that if I'd had the resources and the ability to intervene earlier, they wouldn't have gotten to that point."

Like many officers, Art has a big heart and wants to help, so it's difficult to be on the front lines, seeing the way society often doesn't help people before it's a crisis.

TELL ME WHAT'S WRONG

COMMON DIAGNOSES

SOMETIMES WHEN YOUTH come to see me for counseling, they just want to know "what's wrong" with them. A diagnosis puts a label on a person's experiences. It's kind of like a #hashtag in that it groups similar things together.

A diagnosis can help a person understand what's going on and get the right support. I've heard from many people that they find it comforting to have a diagnosis. It can give a person a sense that they are not alone. This hard time they've been going through is a *thing*. It's got a name. Other people have it. It's not a personal failure. It's an illness. And it can be treated.

On the other hand, a diagnosis can sometimes be unhelpful. It can put the power in the hands of the expert to define what the problem is and how to fix it. A diagnosis can hide the fact that each person is infinitely complex and absolutely unique. Plus, when we really focus on the problem, sometimes we miss all the skills and

MINDSHIFT

ANXIETY CANADA HAS lots of videos, links and other resources. Check out the free MindShift app, which has tools to help you challenge worried thoughts and learn strategies to chill out: anxietycanada.com

strengths a person has. A diagnosis can also cover up the underlying trauma that needs to be healed. Or it can conceal the social causes behind a painful experience. Sometimes I wish I could diagnose a person's school or family or world as the thing that's broken.

When I'm talking with young people, we find language that makes sense to them to describe the problem. Instead of using medical language, I've had youth give the problem names like "The Swirling Hurling Void" or "The Big Angst Eater" or "The Gnar Zone." Sometimes being a bit playful and coming up with a creative name for the problem helps to separate the problem from the person. It helps send the message that you're not the problem, the problem is the problem. And it's something we can tackle together. For example, we can figure out what gives "The Gnar Zone" power and what takes its power away.

That said, this chapter is going to look at some of the common mental health diagnoses that are out there. Just remember, no one is able to be the expert on someone else's life. Also remember that you don't need a diagnosis to get support or to work on finding more healthy ways to cope with difficult thoughts and emotions.

A research team based at Foundry Vancouver-Granville found that trauma-sensitive yoga is helpful for young people struggling with depression, anxiety and PTSD. "Trauma-sensitive" means that the yoga instructor has special training in ways to make the yoga experience feel safer for trauma survivors—for example, by always giving participants choice and control over their own bodies.

ANXIETY

#DANGERDANGER #FIREALARM #FREAKING

nxiety comes in many forms, but all types of anxiety involve the brain signaling "DANGER!" when there's no danger. Or when the danger is small in comparison with how intense it feels. Feeling a bit anxious in new or stressful situations is common. A small amount of stress can actually help us focus and prepare for something difficult, like getting up on stage or running a race. But when our stress response gets big and overwhelming, it can get in the way of doing everyday things.

Generalized anxiety disorder is when a person is constantly nervous and on edge, filled with worry about daily things. Often uncontrollable worries are accompanied by physical symptoms like headaches, stomachaches, muscle tension and difficulty sleeping and concentrating.

Social anxiety disorder is an intense fear of being judged by others. Again, most of us have some fears about looking or sounding stupid. It's pretty common to be worried about speaking in front of a crowd or to replay something you said or did and worry about how it came across. Social anxiety disorder is when a person's fear about what others think gets so overpowering that it leads them to avoid social situations. Sometimes it's so intense that it prevents people from going to school or work or even getting out of the house at all.

A *panic attack* is when the body goes into a sudden, full-on fight-or-flight response. There's a massive rush of adrenaline and the person's heart starts pounding and their breathing gets fast and shallow. Sometimes panic attacks are triggered by specific situations, but often they come out of the blue. *Panic disorder* is diagnosed when a person suffers from unexpected and uncontrollable panic attacks and starts to dread them. The worry about having a panic attack causes the person to avoid going out and doing things they used to enjoy.

All forms of anxiety are very treatable. People can learn skills to calm the body, through mindfulness, biofeedback, visualizations, exposure and breathing techniques. Counseling can help people better understand the relationships between their thoughts, emotions and actions and learn to overcome their fears.

Some people experience a low mood and sluggishness during the winter when the days get shorter and we tend to spend less time outdoors. Getting outside more can help. For some, it's more severe, and the decrease in sunshine leads to major depression year after year. A doctor may recommend taking Vitamin D supplements, using a light that imitates the sun or taking antidepressants.

DEPRESSION

#INTHEDUMPS #GREYCLOUDS #LOWDOWN

E*veryone feels down* from time to time. Sometimes people get stuck in a major slump. Depression can be brought on by life events, or sometimes it slides in with no obvious cause. It feels like unrelenting sadness, a profound empty numbness, or grating irritability that doesn't let up. Whatever the mood, it's not something that a person can just snap out of.

Depression is often also accompanied by fatigue, sleeplessness or sleeping way too much, a lack of appetite or eating way too much, and difficulty concentrating on anything. When a person is depressed, they are unable to enjoy things they once found fun. Often, they are consumed by feelings of guilt and failure. Thoughts can feel slow, muddy and dark. Hopelessness can get so overpowering that for some, death can seem like the only escape.

When you're in the middle of depression, it can be hard to believe things will get better. Sometimes we need encouragement from others who have hope. If you're in a dark place, there is help. With support, life can start to look brighter.

BIPOLAR

#MOODSWINGS #ROLLERCOASTER #OVERTHETOP

Bipolar disorder is a condition where a person has trouble regulating big ups and downs. There are a number of types of bipolar, but usually it involves both **mania** and depression.

Mania is a heightened state of feeling really ramped up and euphoric or extremely irritable. When people are manic, they often feel grandiose, meaning they are extremely overconfident, thinking that they have superpowers or that they could get away with almost anything. Manic episodes often involve needing little or no sleep, and having boundless energy and flights of ideas. People experiencing mania can get obsessive about a project or swept up in risky things, like spending tons of money, sleeping around or driving at breakneck speeds.

Mania is quite extreme and not just a super happy mood. According to the DSM, to qualify as a manic episode, the symptoms have to last for at least a week. If a high mood lasts only four days and isn't quite as severe, it's called hypomania.

ART AND MADNESS?

Kurt Cobain

VINCENT VAN GOGH, the brilliant painter. Virginia Woolf, the iconic feminist writer. Robin Williams, the adorable comedian. Kurt Cobain, the dark king of grunge. Kate Spade, the charismatic fashion designer. The list of creatives who have died by suicide could go on and on. But is the stereotype of the tormented artist an overhyped myth or a sad fact?

A recent review of 36 studies showed that people who have a mood disorder aren't more likely to be creative, but people who have bipolar disorder are. This may be because during an "up" mood it's possible to be really productive. On the other hand, if you experience a chronic low mood, chances are you will be less creative and less productive.

While having a mood disorder doesn't make you creative, being creative means you are more likely to experience a mood disorder. The research doesn't pinpoint the cause but says it's likely because living an artist's life leads to more uncertainty, stress and financial instability than the conventional nine-to-five path. Think of musicians, comics and actors who have to travel and survive gig to gig, often paid very little, without a clear path to success. Or even just being someone who puts their feelings out there could lead to being labeled as depressed or unstable.

Kate Spade

Artists sometimes worry that if they go to therapy, get sober or take meds, their creative spark will go away. But artists who are healthy and happy can still make amazing work. Besides, being depressed or addicted can really get in the way of getting any art done.

Some people with bipolar disorder will cycle between depressive states and manic states. These episodes can be years apart, or sometimes a person might rapid-cycle in the course of a week or even a day. People have also described mixed states where they experience high and low symptoms all at once.

Big mood swings can be confusing and hard to deal with. Finding the right supports, whether through a doctor, mental health professional or peer, can help a person get back to feeling grounded and stable.

LEE'S STORY

Lee Thomas has lapis lazuli eyes, a pixie smile and a spiky, blond crop cut. Their eyebrows seem perpetually raised in excitement. Lee is sauve, political and sparkly. They prize their "truly gay" jean jacket/grey hoodie combo, and their Twitter bio proclaims, "professionally crazy, queer for fun." Lee is a mental health advocate and educator who lives in Fredericton, New Brunswick.

Lee remembers hating high school in the small northern Alberta town where they grew up. When Facebook memories from back then pop up, Lee says they're always a bit shocked at how cutthroat people's comments to each other were. "We were friends," Lee says, "but we didn't really know how to support each other. We showed affection by being horrible and insulting to each other." Lee also describes the town as super homophobic.

Lee started wrestling in Grade 6. They were a fierce competitor and would work out twice a day plus go full-out at wrestling practice. But, Lee says, they had a constant voice running in their head: *You're not good enough, not smart enough, not strong enough, not pretty enough, not* anything *enough.* And this was torture.

Lee remembers that before a wrestling tournament they would get obsessed with "making weight." This involved not eating for a few days and restricting water intake. On the way to tournaments, they wore garbage bags under their sweatpants and sweatshirt and turned the SUV into a sauna to sweat off as much weight as possible. The goal was to weigh in at just under your weight category cutoff.

Looking back, Lee can see that what was normalized as part of the sport turned into an eating disorder that ruled their life for years. Lee managed to keep up good grades, friendships, athletics and student council, and yet, underneath the mask, they were not okay.

Lee says that sometime in Grade 8, they snapped. In a trance, they started bingeing on all the food that they could get their hands on. Then they puked. Guilt and self-hatred burned in their head. Trying to escape the awful feelings, they started cutting. There was a rush of relief, and then the old horrible feelings of self-hatred flooded back in. This became the daily cycle that followed them into their university years—starve, binge, purge, cut.

"Life was getting so scary," Lee says, "but it was even more scary to get help." Lee didn't even know recovery was possible. That's why they share their story now—to let others know it's possible to get help, to get well.

NOT GOOD ENOUGH

Lee sees now that it was so easy to hide partly because in a fatphobic society, thinness and athleticism are seen as noble, as signs of hard work, discipline and moral superiority. While it's often assumed that people with eating disorders are women who are after a hyper-feminine, fashion-model look, Lee wanted an androgynous look. So for a long time nobody suspected that Lee was struggling.

Lee describes themself as "recovering," not "recovered." Recovery isn't an end state; it's a process of self-discovery. Lee is working on loving their body and says that's probably always going to be a work in progress.

Lee
/li/
noun
1. VP Internal of the Student Union
2. Proctor, peer mentor, and activist
3. Dinosaur enthusiast
4. ~~Living with an eating disorder and depression~~

The #MyDefinition campaign, started by Lee Thomas at the University of New Brunswick, aims to make campuses more welcoming to students with mental health challenges.

Lee now teaches Mental Health First Aid and runs a body-image boot camp for youth that challenges all the body-negative messages that come at us from movies, social media, friends and almost everywhere. "It's okay to be real and flawed," Lee says. "You're still worthy of love."

Lee has been given a number of mental health diagnoses over the years, including depression, anxiety, ***bulimia nervosa*** and bipolar disorder. In some ways, Lee found being diagnosed comforting. It meant that other people took their struggles more seriously. Suddenly these struggles were legit. And yet, Lee says, "Your experience of the world doesn't really change based on the label they give you." Each person's experience is unique. Even more importantly, Lee is adamant that each person is always so much more than a diagnosis.

Lee

ON BIPOLAR AND WHAT "NORMAL" MEANS

" **I'D LIKE TO** remind everyone that when you say things like 'Wow, I never would have guessed you had bipolar!' usually the unspoken second part of that sentence is 'because you seem so normal.'

Bipolar disorder doesn't look or act a certain way. Some people with bipolar can't get out of bed. Some can. Some people with bipolar disorder take meds. Some don't. Some people with bipolar disorder can't work. Some can. Some people with bipolar disorder have psychosis. Some don't. And here's the thing— one isn't inherently better than the other.

Normal means something totally different to each person. Sometimes I might totally fit your definition of normal, and sometimes I might not—and that might be because of bipolar disorder symptoms, and it might not be at all. Bipolar disorder or not, we all have our personality quirks and our own demons that we're working through, and our value should not be based on how well we hide those things.

My worst nightmare is being held up as an example in a way that further marginalizes other people—there's a fine line between 'They did it, so you can do it too!' and 'They did it, so why can't you?!' We can be a community, we can talk about our shared struggles and successes, without allowing ourselves to be pitted against one another."

That's why Lee started the #MyDefinition campaign. Here's the key message: "Your mental health is a part of you, but it does not define you." The campaign breaks down **stigma** by making posters that feature real people living with mental illness. Underneath the person's name is a list of "definitions" that capture things like the person's interests, talents and values. The last definition is their mental health diagnosis. And it's crossed out.

PSYCHOSIS

#BRAINTRICKS #TANGLED #WHATSREAL

P sychosis is when a person's brain gets disconnected from reality. It makes it difficult to tell what's real and what isn't real. Two of the main symptoms are delusions and hallucinations. Psychosis can occur as part of many different illnesses, including brief psychotic disorder, schizophrenia, schizoaffective disorder, bipolar, depression and dementia. It can also be triggered by street drugs and medications.

Delusions are beliefs that seem true to the person experiencing them but bizarre or totally false to almost everyone else. Sometimes people with psychosis think that they can read other people's minds or that government agents have tapped into their thoughts. Sometimes they believe that random things, like a chip bag on the street or a billboard slogan, are special signs giving them directions. Grandiose delusions are beliefs that one has extraordinary, godlike powers. With paranoid delusions, the person thinks that others are plotting to harm them or are following them or spying on them.

Hallucinations involve seeing, hearing or smelling things that no one else can detect. These can be very mild, like seeing quick movements in peripheral vision or hearing barely discernible whispers.

REALITY SELF-CHECK

IF YOU'RE WONDERING if you might be experiencing symptoms of psychosis, you can use this online self-check quiz: **foundrybc.ca/ quiz/reality-check**. Remember, it's always worthwhile to consult with a doctor or mental health professional if you have concerns about your mental health.

In fact, when we're tired or anxious, these kinds of tricks of perception can be quite common and are not that concerning. For people with full-blown psychosis, however, hallucinations can be intense, frightening or unrelenting. Some people suffer a barrage of voices that makes it feel like they are continually caught in an agitated, noisy crowd. Some people hear voices arguing or commanding them to do specific tasks. Sometimes the voices may be friendly, sometimes cruel and hostile.

Schizophrenia is an illness characterized by periods of psychosis in which hallucinations and delusions make it difficult to function. Brain changes can result in disorganized thinking and speech.

Negative symptoms also have a big effect on people with schizophrenia. *Negative* here refers to the loss of behaviors that are common for most people. For example, many people diagnosed with schizophrenia have a limited ability to express emotion. Some people speak in a monotone, make hardly any facial expressions and rarely make eye contact. Another negative symptom is frequently being speechless. I remember Tina used to call me and want to talk, but no words would come. It was as if words had completely flown out of her head.

Another common negative symptom is the loss of motivation. This can have a really big effect on a person's ability to work, socialize or do things they used to enjoy. People can even lose the motivation to shower or to do basic self-care.

Psychosis can be a very frightening experience. Fearing being seen as weird, people can become secretive about the strange things they are experiencing. Psychosis can affect someone's ability to even recognize that something is wrong with the way they are thinking—this is often called **lack of insight**. It's not a deliberate avoidance of reality but rather an inability to accurately perceive one's own situation. Imagine how scary and difficult it is to reach for help if you can't understand what is happening and you're suspicious that others are out to get you.

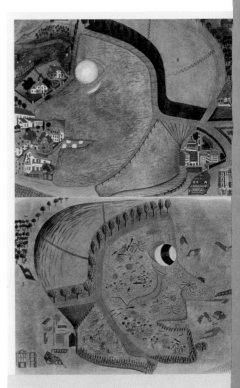

August Natterer was a German electrician who, in his drawings, tried to capture the "10,000 images" he experienced in one half-hour-long hallucination.

Research shows that if people get help early, psychosis is very treatable. Often treatment involves taking medications and learning coping skills. Early treatment increases the chance of making a full recovery.

HEARING VOICES

ELEANOR LONGDEN DESCRIBES sitting outside her parents' bedroom with a plastic fork because the voices in her head had instructed her to protect her parents from danger. All she had was a plastic fork because she had been self-harming and all the other cutlery had been hidden.

In a much-watched TED Talk, Eleanor says that when she turned to friends and professionals for help, everyone assumed that hearing voices equaled insanity. The more professionals she saw, the more anxious she was about the voices. As she became more convinced that she was ill, the voices grew more and more aggressive. Eventually she was hospitalized and diagnosed with schizophrenia.

Today Eleanor is a research psychologist and a manager at the Psychosis Research Unit in Manchester, England. Eleanor now believes that when people hear voices, it can be helpful to explore what the voices are saying rather than just suppressing them with medication. While the more common medical opinion is that voices are disconnected from reality, Eleanor believes that each voice she heard was related to unresolved trauma. She says that when she started listening to them with compassion, she began to understand that they had deeper meaning and could be helpful guides.

Eleanor has been active in the Hearing Voices Movement, a worldwide network of people and groups who believe hearing voices doesn't neces-sarily mean someone is mentally ill. They think of voices as a part of human diversity—something to be paid attention to rather than medicated, and often a survival strategy or a sane reaction to insane circumstances.

Some research suggests that culture plays a role in whether voices are experienced as good or bad. The way people think and feel about their voices may change the tone of the voices and what sorts of things they say. Researchers at Stanford University found that people from Ghana and India were more likely to report that the voices they heard were positive, whereas Americans never thought of their voices as good and were more likely to describe them as hateful and harassing. While more research is needed, the study observed that the African and Indian voice hearers found their voices to be more like friends or family, or like annoying roommates who you have to learn to respect and live with. More often, they described their voices as comforting companions instead of the sign of a broken mind.

Unity is a Toronto-based charity where hip-hop artists share their passions and skills with young people. Learning spoken word, break-dancing, beatboxing and graffiti gives youth confidence, a sense of belonging and an outlet to express their emotions. Last year, more than 70 percent of youth who participated in Unity programs said that it improved their mental health.

PTSD

#TRIGGERWARNING #FLASHBACKS #LEAVINGMYBODY

When someone has experienced something terrifying, feelings of helplessness and distress can continue to live on in their body. Many people who experience a traumatic event will have difficulty coping for a time, but with support from others and good self-care, they recover. When the symptoms of trauma are severe enough to interfere with daily life and last for more than one month, a person may be diagnosed with post-traumatic stress disorder (PTSD).

With PTSD, anxiety runs so high that the person may be very jumpy or irritable, or have sudden explosive outbursts that seem to come out of nowhere. Intrusive memories or flashbacks can cause the person to try to avoid any reminders of the trauma. Changes in mood can include feeling numb, detached and unable to feel close to others.

Some people feel like their own self is fragmented, unrecognizable or not even real. When things get stressful, they can even feel as if they have left their body and are looking down on themselves from a distance. Or the world around them might seem unreal, foggy or dreamlike. Being detached from your sense of self or the world around you is called *dissociation* and can be one of the body's ways of seeking safety.

Trauma therapies and body-oriented therapies are often very helpful. People can learn mindfulness and grounding strategies to regain a sense of safety and calm.

BODY IMAGE AND EATING

#URGES #PERFECTLYME #BOPOWARRIOR

When some people look in the mirror, they hate what they see. They may think they are fat and ugly when that's not what others see at all. Eating disorders involve unrealistic thoughts about one's body and an unhealthy relationship with eating and sometimes exercise. Eating disorders are fueled by a culture that glamorizes unattainable body ideals in movies, TV, magazines and social media. Eating disorders can affect people of any gender, not just girls.

Not everyone who is dissatisfied with their looks develops an eating disorder. An eating disorder often involves a combination of low self-worth, perfectionistic thinking and a strong desire to look a certain way. Sometimes people see their body as the enemy that must be punished and controlled. Eating disorders can lead to life-threatening health problems, including heart and kidney failure.

Disordered eating can involve restricting calories, binge eating, purging food after eating and over-exercising. Some common diagnoses are **anorexia nervosa**, bulimia nervosa and **binge eating disorder.** When an unhealthy pattern takes over a person's life, it can get pretty scary and have serious health consequences.

The sooner a person gets help the better. Seeing a doctor is often a good place to begin.

OCD
#CHECKCHECKCHECKING #INTRUDERS #ONREPEAT

Obsessive-compulsive disorder (OCD) involves obsessions or compulsions and often both.

Obsessions are unwanted thoughts that break into your mind like intruders. People with OCD usually know these thoughts

"FREEDOM FROM UNWANTED THOUGHTS IS A GREAT RELIEF."

are irrational, but they can't control them. This can cause a lot of distress. Obsessive thoughts can be about anything. A couple of common ones are fearing contamination by germs or fearing something bad will happen if things aren't kept in a precise order. Some people experience intense fears of hurting others or blurting out something horrible even though they never would want to hurt anyone.

Compulsions are repetitive rituals a person feels driven to perform in an attempt to get their obsessive thoughts to go away. Some common compulsions are needing to wash one's hands repeatedly, counting things, checking things again and again or performing a precise series of actions to prevent a disaster. Compulsions follow very rigid rules and can actually become stronger the more frequently they are repeated.

While many people have a mild need to check things or keep things orderly, a diagnosis of OCD is only given when a person's obsessions and compulsions are so overpowering that they take up a huge amount of mental energy and impact their ability to enjoy life or get things done.

Treatment from a mental health professional can help decrease the intensity and impact of OCD symptoms. Finding freedom from unwanted thoughts and compulsive urges is a great relief and can give a person energy to get back to living a full life.

BORDERLINE

#BIGFEELS #DONTLEAVEME #ROLLERCOASTER

Borderline personality disorder is a diagnosis that describes a pattern of having big emotional reactions, stormy relationships and an unstable sense of self. All of us are social beings and need to feel connected to others, so it makes sense that part of being human is fear of abandonment. However, some people are super feelers and their emotional reactions are more intense and harder to soothe. Research also shows that people who have the symptoms of this diagnosis have usually experienced trauma.

For people who are highly sensitive, everyday conflicts can feel like life-or-death situations. They can easily feel betrayed or rejected. They can feel a ton of shame, and also direct a lot of blame at others. These painful feelings can result in impulsive behaviors, like driving recklessly, using substances unsafely, cutting off relationships or running away. Some people are chronically suicidal or frequently injure themselves.

Borderline is a diagnosis that has often been misunderstood even by professionals who work in the field. People with this label have been unfairly judged as attention-seeking, manipulative and hard to help. However, the research shows that when people diagnosed with borderline are treated with compassion and respect and given

"ALL OF US ARE SOCIAL
AND NEED TO
FEEL CONNECTED
TO OTHERS."

adequate treatment, they can tame their runaway emotions and build stable, meaningful lives.

Treatment often involves therapy where people learn skills for tolerating distress, calming emotions and building satisfying relationships. Where there is underlying trauma, counseling that focuses on healing it can also be very helpful.

SUBSTANCE USE
#JUSTONEMORE #CANTSTOP #EASEUP

We all have ways of coping with stress and emotional pain, some more healthy than others. Some people binge-watch movies or exercise a ton or bury themselves in work. For others it might be gaming until all hours of the night or gambling until their money runs out. For others, it's a chemical fix.

There are almost as many different substances that produce mind-altering effects as there are reasons why people use them, from loosening up to escaping major troubles. It can start out fun and turn into something risky and unpredictable, and even life-threatening.

SOME SIGNS THAT substance use is getting sketchy:

- you're using substances to deal with another problem
- you're mixing substances
- you're ramping up your use
- you're using in riskier ways
- you're using at times when you really need a clear head
- you're neglecting things you really care about

It's no secret that people use drugs and alcohol to try to feel good. The substances people use all have the ability to activate the brain's reward system. The brain's pleasure response can be so intense and lightning-fast that people start to neglect other parts of life in order to get a high.

When substance use gets problematic, there is often an underlying change in the brain circuits caused by the substance. These brain changes can cause intense cravings and persist even after the person has detoxed the substance out of their body.

NATURAL HIGHS

PLASTERED, WASTED—20 YEARS AGO
Icelandic teens were known for heavy alcohol and drug use. Today they're getting high in healthier ways.

Binge drinking used to be considered no big deal among Icelandic teens. In 1998, when asked about their drinking in the last 30 days, almost half of the youth surveyed said that they had been drunk. Over the last 20 years, that has dropped to only 5 percent. This is a big shift.

Iceland's policy-makers realized that people primarily use drugs and alcohol to reduce stress. But there are other ways to get the brain to create its own stress-relieving chemical alterations, through things like music, dance and sports.

Plus, they realized the research shows that warning kids about the dangers of drugs and alcohol doesn't work. The key is to get youth hooked on natural highs so they are never really tempted by artificial highs.

So the Icelandic government created a national plan to get kids having fun and feeling connected. They educated parents about the importance of spending lots of quality time with their kids, and over the years family time doubled. The government also created a huge variety of organized sports, music, art and dance programs and gave each child a good chunk of money to pay for fun activities so everyone could have access, no matter what their family income.

While Iceland's rates of teenage drinking were once the highest in Europe, they are now the lowest, and promoting natural highs is taking off in other countries.

With the recent opioid crisis, overdose fatalities have skyrocketed. Supervised injection sites provide people with clean needles and a safe place to use drugs. These sites have been proven to reduce overdose deaths and reduce infections. Plus, people who use these sites have the opportunity to connect with health-care workers and social workers if they want further help.

Substance use can have a big effect on teenagers. Because the teenage brain is still developing, it may be more affected—and more permanently affected—by drugs and alcohol.

As substance use becomes problematic, it can become harder and harder to control the impulse to use, and a person will start using increasing amounts and using more frequently. At this point, the body has gotten used to a steady supply. Cravings can be so strong that it's impossible to think of anything else.

The signs and symptoms of **intoxication** and **withdrawal** vary depending on the substance. But when substance use starts affecting relationships and the ability to function in day-to-day life, that's a signal that it's time to get help.

Like any mental health problem, a person's vulnerability to substance use can be affected by both their biology and their circumstances in life. When life is difficult or unfair or highly stressful, drugs and alcohol can be harder to resist. Research shows that the substance use rates for people who have experienced violence or sexualized abuse—especially during childhood—are particularly high.

Harm reduction is a philosophy that accepts that people who use substances are often unable or unwilling to quit. A harm reduction approach supports people in being as healthy as possible and in ways that work for them. Harm reduction can include things like using safer substances, using clean needles or using at a safe injection site so you're not alone in case of an overdose. Or it can be simply using less. It can mean going to a party with friends and making sure you keep an eye on each other and leave together. It can mean alternating between beer and club soda. It can mean setting a limit on how much you drink or how many times a month you party. Anything that keeps you safer and healthier is a good thing.

DRUG COCKTAILS

ONE OF THE most dangerous things you can do is mix alcohol, prescription medications and street drugs. *Drug Cocktails* is a resource that helps explain the effects and interactions of different substances so people can make safer decisions. For more information, check out **drugcocktails.ca**

SELF-INJURY

#IHURT #ICANTEVEN #INSIDEOUT

Self-injury can be a coping strategy when a person doesn't know how else to deal with overwhelming feelings. Some people hurt themselves by cutting, burning, scratching or hitting themselves. Sometimes self-injury is a way to feel *something* when a person is feeling totally numbed out. Sometimes it's a way of communicating to others just how much pain is under the surface. Sometimes it's a way to punish oneself. Usually when a person self-injures, it is

SELF-INJURY
OUTREACH AND SUPPORT

IF YOU WANT TO read stories of recovery or learn more about how to cope with urges to self-injure, take a look at the *Self-injury Outreach and Support* website: **sioutreach.org**

not with the intent to die, although sometimes people do also have suicidal thoughts when they are in a state of high distress. For some, self-injury is actually a way of staying alive.

Self-injury might give a person a little hit of relief, but that relief is usually very short-lived and the painful feelings or numbness returns. Counseling or group therapy can be a good way to process over-whelming feelings and learn safer coping strategies. Many people find it helpful to experiment with other ways to shift their headspace, with things like physical exercise, grounding, mindfulness or yoga.

SUICIDAL THOUGHTS
#HELP

hen things get really overwhelming, sometimes people start to wonder if life is worth living or if the world would be better off if they didn't exist. Hope gets especially thin when people can't find the help they need.

Suicide can be a tough one to talk about. Some people think it's a sin. Some people say suicide is selfish. Or they say we have to keep

"MANY PEOPLE FIND IT HELPFUL TO EXPERIMENT WITH OTHER WAYS TO SHIFT THEIR HEADSPACE, WITH THINGS LIKE PHYSICAL EXERCISE, GROUNDING, MINDFULNESS OR YOGA."

I'M HERE FOR YOU

it hush-hush or everyone will run out and do it. But silence doesn't help. Among young people ages 15 to 24, suicide is the most common cause of death. This is really important stuff to talk about.

When I was a teenager, one of my closest friends told me she was thinking of killing herself. She couldn't tell me what was going on, but I guessed something horrible had happened to her. At that time, she begged me not to tell anyone about her suicidal thoughts and I kept her secret. I realize now I should have got help.

I'm grateful that she eventually talked to a counselor. But I wonder if she suffered for longer than she needed to because I was scared.

I would have been devastated if she had ended her life. While I know she might have been mad at me if I had broken her trust, I realize now that she would have forgiven me. She would've eventually understood that it was my love for her that made me decide to share her secret and get help.

Many of the youth I've worked with have experienced suicidal thoughts when life was difficult. This isn't weird or wrong. It's probably more common than we think. Most of these youth don't really want to die—they want the awful stuff they're experiencing to stop.

When life feels unbearable or meaningless, it's understandable to seek relief from the suffering. Our brains are problem-solving devices, and sometimes when we can't come up with a way to fix things, our brain pops up suicide as the solution. Some youth tell me that just thinking about suicide can be relieving. It's like having an escape hatch, even if you know you don't want to use it right now.

There's a spectrum in the intensity of suicidal thoughts. I have experienced the wish to just not wake up, to not have to face another day. These thoughts can be fleeting or it might be possible to intentionally focus your mind on other things. But it's still a big sign that things are not okay and it's time to get help.

Sometimes suicidal thoughts can be more intense. They can be vivid and overwhelming. They can progress to planning how to die. Sometimes the thoughts can be nearly impossible to ignore. When emotions are high or your head feels fuzzy and suicidal thoughts are taking over, it can be hard to make good decisions or figure out what to do. When someone's head is stuck in suicidal thoughts, they need urgent help to find other solutions to the pain.

If this is happening to you or a friend, it's crucial to get help now. Let a trusted adult know, call a crisis line or get to the hospital. Don't go through this alone. Reach out. There are people who want to help. And who *can* help.

WHAT MAKES A LIFE FEEL LIVABLE?

The desire to die means something needs to change for life to feel livable again. What that something is can be very individual. But often the desire to die points to the very things that make a life worth living—the need for love, belonging, respect, purpose and meaning.

Research on suicide has focused on identifying risk factors—the things that can statistically make death by suicide more likely. These are based on studies of large populations. Some common risk factors are a serious physical or mental illness, experiences of violence, and problems with drugs or alcohol. A major loss or life change, like a death or a divorce or a move, can also feel unbearable. Things can pile up and feel like too much.

Often it's the social context of people's lives that makes life feel unlivable. Discrimination and injustice can be really hurtful, and suicide is more common among those who identify as Indigenous, people of color or LGBTQ2S+. Suicidal thoughts or acts can be seen as a response to injustice. A way of protesting mistreatment. A way of saying, "I can't live with this! I need a better world!"

One practical thing that makes suicide more likely is if someone has easy access to a way to hurt themselves. This can be a pretty simple thing to change: keep dangerous things like guns, sharps and pills locked away. Usually, with time, suicidal thoughts will lessen in intensity. So keeping dangerous things hard to access means the person will have more time for the suicidal thoughts to fade and for reconnecting with the things that make their life worth living.

Keep in mind that risk isn't destiny. Risk factors describe populations that have higher suicide rates but don't describe an individual person's risk of dying by suicide. Each person can be affected very differently by the circumstances of their life. And anyone could be at risk of suicide if their pain feels unbearable.

Doctors in Canada and elsewhere are prescribing time outside for patients. Spending time in nature has been shown to reduce anxiety, depression, ADHD and aggressive behavior.

On the flip side, things that make life worth living help us get through tough times. These are often called protective factors. A willingness to seek help and learn coping skills can be protective. Good friends, positive role models, strong family connections and a sense of belonging at home, at school or in the community can keep a person connected with life. A strong cultural identity or spiritual beliefs can also provide a sense of belonging and meaning. Opportunities to learn, have fun and connect with nature are also essential ingredients for a life that feels worth it.

WARNING SIGNS

When someone is getting to that point of feeling that life isn't worth living, they often show warning signs. These are red flags that say they need urgent help. The American Association of Suicidology recommends a simple phrase for remembering the warning signs: IS PATH WARM. This stands for:

Ideation—Do they have thoughts of wanting to die? Are they saying things like "people would be better off without me" or "there is nothing worth living for" or "I can't take it anymore"? Are they posting about suicide on social media?

Substance use—Are they using drugs or drinking more than usual?

Purposelessness—Are they feeling like there is no purpose in life or no reason for living?

Anxiety—Are they showing signs of intense anxiety or feeling overwhelmed?

Trapped—Are they feeling trapped, like there is no way out?

Hopelessness or Helplessness—Are they feeling like things will never get better? Are they feeling helpless and don't know what to do?

Withdrawal—Are they avoiding family or friends? Are they losing interest in hanging out or doing things they used to enjoy?

Anger—Are they expressing a lot of anger?

Recklessness—Are they doing risky things that they usually wouldn't do?

Mood changes—Are they having big mood swings?

HOW TO HELP A FRIEND

Listen—Listen without judgment. Don't minimize how they are feeling or try to convince them that it's not so bad. Instead, let them know you hear the emotion. You might say something like "It sounds like you're feeling really overwhelmed." Or "You sound so down and I'm worried about you."

R U OK?

WANNA TALK?

. . .

I'M HERE FOR YOU.

Ask—Ask if they are thinking about suicide. It's okay to ask directly: "Are you thinking of killing yourself?" It's a myth that talking about suicide might lead someone to take their own life. Talking openly signals that it's okay to talk about hard stuff and increases the chances that a person will get help.

Reassure—Don't offer advice. Don't tell them how great their life is. Just tell them you care. You can simply say, "Thank you for telling me. I want to help."

Reach out—If you think a friend is having suicidal thoughts, ask for help from a trusted adult. Don't carry this alone. Don't delay. Notify a parent, a teacher or a counselor, or call a crisis line or 9-1-1. Remember to take good care of yourself too. Supporting a friend can be tough, and you may need to talk to someone.

Stay connected—This probably isn't a one-time emergency. People need ongoing support. Check in. Send them smiley faces, hearts and playful kitten vids or comedy mash-ups. Drop by. Go out for fries. Even if they're not able to respond, keep on reminding them you care.

INSTEAD OF SAYING...

It's not that bad. You're so _ _ _ _ _ _ _ .
(cool, popular, talented, smart, lucky, etc.)

I know exactly how you feel!

Chill! Cheer up. It's all gonna be okay.

Others have it a lot worse.

Stop being so dramatic. All you want is attention.

You're not going to off yourself, are you?!

Don't worry, I'll never tell.

SAY SOMETHING LIKE...

It sounds like you've been going through a difficult time. I'm so glad you told me.

How has that been for you?

You're not in this alone. You can talk to me anytime.

That sounds so hard. Is there anything I can do to help?

Are you okay? I'm worried you're really not okay.

Are you thinking of suicide?

I can't keep this a secret. I care about you too much.

stay

Dese'Rae

YOU'RE NOT ALONE. If you experience suicidal thoughts, you can get through this. That is what Dese'Rae L. Stage wants people to know. She is a photographer and a suicide attempt survivor. Dese'Rae has produced the website *Live Through This*, which features the stories and portraits of suicide survivors.

Dese'Rae struggled with anxiety, low mood and self-injury for 10 years before an abusive relationship tipped her into a suicidal crisis. Just in time, paramedics barged into her apartment and whisked her away to the hospital. In the years since then she has picked up her camera and become an accomplished photographer.

Dese'Rae has created an online space where people can talk about their experiences openly and honestly. For some people, suicide is a past experience that is a small part of who they are. For others, their near-death experience has been pivotal and defining. Everyone's story is different. And yet the pain is similar. And so is the courage it takes to find a way to live through it.

"I've collected so many different stories from so many different people," Dese'Rae says. "From tech developers to musicians to people who live on mental health disability. Stories that run the gamut from multiple personality disorder to postpartum depression to sexualized abuse to people who had completely normal childhoods and don't know why they're suicidal."

In each portrait, the person looks directly into your eyes with a gaze both vulnerable and vital. These stories are difficult, but each one is a celebration of survival. Of finding hope. Of life. To read these raw and inspiring stories, check out **livethroughthis.com**

THINGS NOT COVERED

#MORETOTHIS #LIMITS #NEVERSTOPLEARNING

There are so many other struggles and mental health diagnoses that people live with. There isn't space in this book to cover all possible diagnoses, but take a look at the Resources section to find places to look for good information.

Just remember, you don't need to know someone's diagnosis to support them. If you notice that someone is in distress or is acting or speaking in ways that are puzzling, check in with them. Sometimes it helps just to be treated with respect and kindness. Ask them what they need and start there.

5

THE ROAD TO WELLNESS

ON SURVIVING AND THRIVING

AT ONE TIME, mental illness was thought to be a life sentence. But patients and survivors have long fought for a more hopeful approach. The recovery movement thinks of recovery as a personal journey, one that each person gets to define for themselves.

Recovery is based on the idea that each person has the right to figure out their own version of wellness and should be supported by society to do this. Recovery does not equal being cured. It isn't necessarily a perfect state of health. It's when a person gets to decide for themselves what a meaningful, dignified life looks like. Even if a person continues to live with symptoms of mental illness, they can still have a good quality of life and experience wellness.

For some people, recovery involves being supported with various treatment services. For others, it's more about a sense of belonging in their community or being able to pursue work and personal interests. For still others, it's freedom from psychiatric labels and treatments. Recovery is about creating a fulfilling life and charting your own road to wellness.

RESILIENCE

hen emotions get big and hard to handle, you might wonder how you'll ever get through it. Resilience is the ability to cope with challenging experiences and to live a meaningful life even though it's not easy. It doesn't mean it isn't painful or confusing. It just means you are able to get through it.

You wake up feeling down, but you get up anyway, have a shower, eat some breakfast and get out the door. You don't feel great, but you trust that you'll feel better if you do something other than lying in bed all day. That takes some grit.

Resilience isn't something that only amazing, superhero-type people have. It's something we all can learn and practice. Resilience is self-compassion, determination, optimism and the ability to calm yourself, to endure distress, to resist acting impulsively, to put things in perspective and to connect with others.

Resilience also comes from feeling you've got people who care for you and treat you with respect. Some of us are lucky to find this easily in our family or community. Others have to search long and hard.

Each of us needs to feel that we are seen, heard and understood. When you look into the eyes of someone you trust and see kindness and understanding in their face, your nervous system is soothed. Love and belonging builds resilience.

Research shows that loneliness is a major risk factor for dying young. In fact, it rates right up there with smoking in terms of how bad it is for your physical health. Feeling isolated and suffering in silence can also worsen anxiety and depression. Connecting with friends, family or your community is good for your body as well as your sense of well-being.

BREAKING THROUGH SHAME AND STUFF THAT KEEPS US STUCK

heer up! Don't worry! It will all be okay! Ever heard that? Often people try to say nice things to make us feel better. But sometimes (mostly, maybe) these messages make us feel worse. It can make it seem like it's not okay to be down or stressed out or hurting. Not to mention all the social media that makes it look like everyone else is living 100 percent fantastic lives.

Sometimes we give these messages to ourselves: *What's my problem? It's not that bad, I should be okay! I should suck it up! I should try harder!* "Should-ing on yourself" is not usually helpful. It can make you feel like crap. It can make you feel guilty even though what you're going through is just human.

Our minds can go haywire with harsh thoughts like *I'm such a loser, I screw everything up, Nobody cares, What's the point?* Often when we try to push feelings away, they just get bigger. It can get into a spin cycle where the more you try to hide or ignore your feelings, the worse they get.

Talking can help untangle difficult feelings. If you let them out and give them some air, they often start to feel more understandable and more workable.

It's not easy to ask for help. If you're experiencing low motivation, anxiety or hopelessness, it can be very hard to walk in the door of a strange place and talk to a new person. People often feel unsure that they are going to be believed or taken seriously. It can even be difficult to talk to someone you know and trust. One of the major things that keeps people from reaching out is shame.

Shame is that crawl-into-a-hole feeling of being unlovable. It's the idea that *I'm not worth it.* Sometimes shame causes us to pretend to be something we're not, or to desperately try to please others. Sometimes it can make us lash out and heap shame on someone else. Sometimes it causes us to withdraw and hide, or to frantically scramble to do things perfectly. Shame is a pretty toxic force.

Shame often comes with a really harsh inner voice: *If people knew my inner muck, they wouldn't love me.* The pressure of keeping up an act in order to be loved and accepted is exhausting. Giving in to the feeling of unworthiness is isolating.

When I'm not doing well, all I want to do is hide. I feel exhausted, fuzzy-headed and shut-down. My body hurts. Things feel impossible.

Shame can make you feel as if you have been coated in some high-tech material that only lets in the bad stuff. Compliments or kindnesses bounce right off, but insensitive or careless comments stab right in.

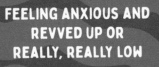

FEELING ANXIOUS AND
REVVED UP OR
REALLY, REALLY LOW

GETTING DOWN
ON YOURSELF FOR
HOW YOU FEEL

*There's something
wrong with me.*

the SPIN CYCLE

FEELING
WORSE

IGNORING OR
HIDING YOUR
FEELINGS

Poof!

Shame is one of the biggest things that keeps us from connecting with others. And yet connecting with others and sharing our pain is actually the best therapy ever.

Brené Brown, a researcher on love and vulnerability, says that belonging is very different from fitting in. Fitting in is figuring out what you need to say, do, look like and so on to be one of the crowd. Belonging is when you get to be yourself—with all your quirks and flaws—and still feel loved and accepted.

Doesn't that sound amazing?

Shame often keeps us from reaching out. But I truly believe that if we can summon the courage to speak the truth about what's going on for us, things can change. We can find connection and belonging.

A recent study shows that being able to forgive yourself and others is linked to better mental health. While more research is needed, this study suggests that people who practice forgiveness decrease their stress levels, which results in greater well-being.

SELF-COMPASSION

EVERY PERSON FEELS "not enough" in some way. Trust me, you're not the only one who feels flawed and unlovable. One of the things I've found to be the best antidote to shame is practicing self-compassion.

Kristin Neff, a researcher on self-compassion, suggests that we all need to practice being kind to ourselves. Practice means you've got to do it over and over again to get better at it. One of the things she suggests is taking little breaks where we just check in with ourselves and try using a kind inside voice instead of a harsh inside voice. Here are four steps she recommends practicing in a quiet moment:

1. **THINK ABOUT** the thing that's difficult for you. What's going on? How is it affecting you? Get in touch with what is hard about it.

2. **GENTLY GET REAL** with yourself by saying *This is so painful for me. I'm really having a tough time.* Or find your own words to acknowledge how you're feeling. Let yourself know your feelings matter.

3. **REMIND YOURSELF** that suffering is a part of being human. You might say something like *It's understandable to feel this way. I'm not the only one. I'm just human.*

4. **MAKE A WISH** or a promise to take good care of yourself. Say something like *I'm going to be gentle and kind to myself. I want to treat myself like I would a close friend. I'm going to take good care of myself.*

You can find guided meditations to listen to on Kristin Neff's website: **selfcompassion.org**

Tunchai

ON REACHING OUT

"**HELLO. MY NAME IS TUNCHAI REDVERS.** I'm Dene and Métis from the Northwest Territories. I'm a poet, a social justice warrior and the cofounder of *We Matter*. I'm here to tell you that life is really hard. And there are hardships that we have to experience in life that seem really unfair. And they are really unfair. But I'm here to tell you that you can get through anything that comes your way.

I was 11 years old when I started having suicidal thoughts. And for many years I had suicidal thoughts. I was bullied really badly. I've been in abusive relationships. I've experienced trauma. I have trauma in my family. I have addiction in my family. When I was 15, I took a lot of pills and I ended up in the hospital. What I learned from that experience is that I didn't want to die. I just wanted to stop hurting. I didn't want to be in pain anymore.

At that time, I didn't know that I had other options. I didn't know that all I had to do was reach out and tell somebody how I was feeling. For my whole life I had kept everything inside of me. And it started to feel really lonely. I felt lonely and empty and weak. But once I started to talk about those things, things got easier. I wasn't on my own. There were suddenly people who loved and cared about me, who were there to support me.

We all have a light and nobody can ever steal your light from you. You are the only person who gets to decide who you are. Nobody else can do that. Nobody can take your light from you. So guard your light."

THE PROS

Sometimes it's helpful to get professionals onboard. For starters, it's important that you find someone you feel comfortable with. The more comfortable you are, the more likely you'll be able to just lay out what's going on.

Trust is important for a good relationship, so professionals are bound by confidentiality. This means they keep your story private and only share your information with your permission, unless there is a very serious safety concern. Confidentiality can be especially important for teenagers, because sometimes you may need to talk about something you just don't feel comfortable with your parents or others in your life knowing.

A family doctor or general practitioner (GP) is often a good place to start. A doctor will be able to do a thorough assessment of your mental and physical health and recommend some next steps.

Psychiatrists have a medical degree, just like a GP, plus they have gone on to get specialized training in the diagnosis and treatment of mental illnesses. Psychiatrists are often used as consultants and will work with other mental health professionals to help treat the most complex cases.

Psychologists have a doctorate in psychology and must be registered with a professional association. Psychologists often provide talk therapy, but they can also do more specialized assessments related to emotional disorders, intellectual or developmental impairments and behavioral problems.

Counselors or therapists are professionals who specialize in talk therapy. They usually have an advanced degree in counseling psychology or social work. Registration with a professional association ensures that they meet a high standard of education and ethical practice.

They often specialize in a particular type of therapy, such as cognitive behavioral therapy, dialectical behavior therapy, body-based therapies, narrative therapy, art therapy, family therapy or nature therapy. When you're looking for a counselor, you can ask them to explain the approach they use and see if it's a good fit for you.

Remember, the most important thing is that you find someone you click with. A good, safe connection with another human being is the most healing thing.

Asante Haughton

ASANTE'S STORY

In 10th grade Asante Haughton stopped hanging out with friends and stopped enjoying school. He had always been a good student. His mom had taught him to read at age three and being a whiz kid had always been his thing. But he no longer cared. He had no motivation. Nobody knew what was going on at home, and he didn't know who to turn to.

Asante's mom had been going to university and working a bunch of low-paying jobs, trying to support her three kids. She was stressed and irritable, but Asante didn't know how bad things really were.

Then one Sunday morning when he was watching the Euro Cup finals with his brothers, a crisis team knocked on the door. His mom was slumped in the bedroom, pills scattered all around her. Bravely, she had called the crisis line and asked for help. That night she was taken to the hospital, given a prescription for antidepressants and sent home.

"It felt like a wrecking ball hit me," Asante remembers. How bad was it? Had she come close to dying? Would the pills help? Who could he turn to or call if she wasn't well?

A few months later, Asante came home from school and found out she was in the hospital again. It hit him that there wasn't going to be a quick fix. His mom was in the hospital for weeks, and this time the pills stayed scattered on the floor. He just couldn't look at them.

Asante's feelings of isolation turned into deep anxiety. He didn't hang out with friends or date or go to parties. He didn't really even talk to anyone. He became very self-conscious about his body, thinking he was too skinny, that his head was too big for his body and his teeth were too crowded and jacked up. Eventually he stopped looking in the mirror altogether.

He was worried that people thought he was weird. It got to the point where he could barely leave the house. "I felt like there was something tremendously wrong with me because I couldn't do what other kids my age were doing," Asante says. "All I knew was something was wrong with Mom. And something was wrong with me."

Back then, Asante didn't understand what was happening. Today, knowing more of his mom's story has helped him understand his own story. "If I told you all the things my mom has been through," Asante says, "you wouldn't believe it." He speaks of her with warm admiration.

Asante's mom grew up in Jamaica in a poor family. They never had a stable place to live and they had to scrounge through garbage

for food. When Asante was three years old, his mom moved with her children to Canada to escape violence and build a new life.

But even after the suicide attempts, the worst was yet to come. Asante could tell that his mom was struggling, but he couldn't quite figure out what was wrong. Even though she was holding down two jobs, it was like she was checked out, in a fog. The look on her face had changed. So had the rhythm of her speech. She started to be afraid that the government and the police were after her for some outstanding student loans. She started forbidding Asante to go certain places and to answer the phone.

"I would try to reason with her but it was just impossible," Asante says. He soon realized that arguing didn't help her become more realistic in her thinking.

Asante's mom started hearing voices and the paranoia increased in intensity. She flushed her reading glasses down the toilet because she thought the authorities could spy on her through them. With a hammer, she destroyed the computer that had her university papers on it. Then she ordered Asante and his brothers to spread the pieces of the computer in random dumpsters across Toronto. Asante rode the bus with a smashed-up computer in his bag, thinking "I'm just going to do this thing that I know doesn't make sense because it will calm her down."

The internet got cut off. The TV got cut off. Asante would steal food and ration it through the week. He'd come straight home from school to spend time with his mom. He would make toast or spaghetti and try to coax her to eat. For months she was barely sleeping or eating. She became so thin you could see her heart beating in her chest.

At the same time, Asante slipped into depression. "I was really sad all the time," he says. "I had no motivation. I stopped doing homework. It was impossible for me to get excited about anything. I didn't know what it was like to have fun anymore. I was still going to school every day, but I had completely disengaged from life. The switch went off and I was kinda done."

Asante turned to writing poetry and rap lyrics. Some of the angry and violent emotions coming out on the page scared him. But this outlet also helped him to get through this time.

One night, Asante and his brothers realized they had to get help. Things were getting scary. It was like their mom was a different person. She was angry and scared of everything. Conspiracies were spinning in her head. When they tried to convince her to go to the hospital, she refused. She threatened to jump off a nearby overpass. Quickly they called 9-1-1.

She was in hospital for months. The doctors said she had been only a week away from dying of starvation. This time, when she was released from hospital, she was connected with a team of professionals. She had been diagnosed with schizoaffective disorder and prescribed antipsychotics. She started to learn how to manage her own mental health.

For Asante, the sense of relief was immense. She was finally getting help. This was the beginning of her recovery. And even though Asante would continue to struggle with depression in his university years, it was the beginning of his recovery too.

He started playing basketball morning, noon and night. He had a coach who believed in him, and the school gym was usually open. He started working out and analyzing games on TV. While he had started Grade 12 without much skill, he ended the year as the team's most valuable player. Basketball helped him meet people and make friends. It was a way of feeling alive again.

Eventually Asante went to get help from a therapist. "She was super real with me," Asante says. "She helped me open up to discover things about myself and my life that I hadn't clued in to. All the things that I thought were wrong with me suddenly had an explanation. They made sense. And that was the beginning of the shame lifting."

Asante encourages people to reach out for support—to a teacher, a counselor, a peer worker or some other trusted person. "When I was younger," he says, "I thought that if I talked to a professional it would mean that I was crazy or that something was fractured or

Stella's Place uses a holistic approach to mental health for young people, combining clinical support with things like employment assistance, opportunities to develop creativity, fitness programs and peer support groups.

broken, and I didn't want to see myself that way." Now he realizes that having a listening ear and someone to help you understand what is going on can be so helpful.

Today Asante is the leader of the peer support training program at Stella's Place, a hub for youth mental health in Toronto. To stay healthy, he makes smoothies and focuses on turning his eye inward, through writing or through just taking a quiet moment. He pays close attention to how relaxed or stressed he is in his body. He is now a lot better at recognizing how he is feeling in the moment.

He tries to remember that even if what he is feeling is intense, it will probably be less intense in three hours or three days or three weeks. "All pain is temporary," he often reminds the people he works with. "It might be really difficult for a while, but you can get through it."

INVOLUNTARY TREATMENT

ONE OF THE MOST EMOTIONALLY and ethically challenging issues in the treatment of mental illness is involuntary treatment. At times a person's brain can be so incapacitated that they are unable to understand their own situation and unable to seek the help they need. If a person is thought to be a "*danger to self or others*," there is often a legal justification for doing something to intervene to keep everyone safe.

The law sets out circumstances under which a person may be admitted to a hospital against their own wishes. In many places, a police officer or a doctor can make the decision that someone needs to go to hospital to be further assessed. Or if a family member or friend is concerned about someone, they can ask a judge to issue a warrant for the police to find the person and take them to hospital. Then, once in hospital, if at least two doctors agree that the person needs urgent treatment to prevent them from harming themselves or others, the patient can be held against their will until they have recovered their ability to make sound decisions and act safely.

Having someone involuntarily admitted—or "committed" or "certified"—can be a very difficult decision. It's stressful to see someone you care about in a severe mental health crisis. Sometimes if a person has had bad experiences in the past or is scared of being locked up, they have a lot of good reasons for not wanting to ask for help. When I have been involved in this process, I have always been troubled by forcing treatment on someone. It can feel like such a violation of trust. But sometimes it might be the only way to keep a person alive.

GOOD HITS

BASICS FOR SURVIVING AND THRIVING

Here are 10 things you can do to lift your mood. Let's get basic. These are good hits that everybody needs:

Move it—When you're feeling sluggish, you might just want to curl up and play dead. But the slugs will take over your body if you let them. To get a jolt of good chemicals, get moving. Even a 10-minute walk can change how you feel. Or put on some music and bop, break-dance or just fling yourself around.

Writing stuff down can help you calm your body, understand your emotions and get perspective.

Get face-to-face—Connect in person. It's easy to hide away or zone out online, but we all need to hang with other people IRL. Pick someone you feel safe and good with. Sometimes it's enough to just be together.

Let your feelings flow—Find someone you can talk to and let it flow. Or pull out a journal and free-write. Or sketch or just mess around with color. Or let yourself have a big cry or beat on a pillow. Surf the wave of your feelings and know they're real and important.

Feed the life force—Eat something delicious and healthy. Food can be so comforting. Let your body know you want to take care of it.

Slow down—Give yourself the night off and do something soothing. Listen to calming music. Take a hot bath. Cuddle with a pet. For the moment, just focus on something relaxing.

Get outside—Find something in nature to stare at. It might be a sunset or a little wild plant growing in the crack of a sidewalk. Hang with it. Notice the light and the feel of the air. Wonder at it. Isn't it amazing how life is tenacious and intricate and flowing around us all the time?

Conk out—Sleep is essential because it's when your brain and body heal. Make it your mission to get at least eight hours each night. Devise a bedtime routine to help you wind down. Shut down screens a few hours before bed because they beam blue light into your eyeballs, telling your brain to wake up. Take a hot shower, make a herbal tea, have a little snack, listen to soothing music or a podcast, then tuck in.

Lighten up—We all need fun and a few laughs. Even if it's hard to imagine having fun right now, write a list of anything that you enjoyed at some point in your life. Then pick one thing to do each day. Even if you don't feel like it. If you're having trouble thinking of something, google *kittens* or *puppies* or *dancing babies*.

Do something nice for someone else—Sometimes a good way to get out of your own head is to think about others. It might be something practical or just a little note to let them know you care. Bet you can't do this without feeling a little better.

Do what matters—What is it that you really care about? Do that!

Science shows that exercise that gets your heart pumping lifts your mood. Aerobic exercise makes the brain release endorphins. Weight lifting has also been proven to boost mood and motivation.

6

CANDID AND COURAGEOUS

IT'S TIME TO TALK

SELENA GOMEZ CUT short her 2015 Revival World Tour to get help for anxiety and depression. When she won Favorite Female Artist at the 2016 American Music Awards, she said, "I had everything and I was absolutely broken inside." She struggled with loneliness and poor self-esteem. She had panic attacks before and after getting on stage. Even though she had millions of fans, she felt that she wasn't good enough. Through therapy, practicing mindfulness and taking a break from social media, Gomez found her way to feeling healthy and grounded.

Michael Phelps, the most decorated Olympic athlete of all time, with 28 medals, 23 of them gold, recently decided it was time to

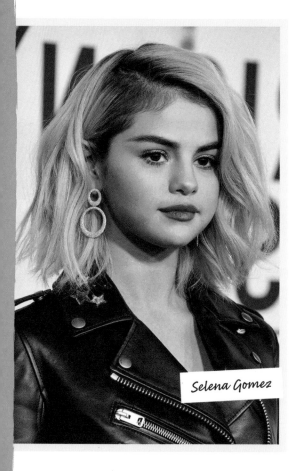

Selena Gomez

talk about his mental health. On his way to competing in his fifth Olympic games, Phelps was charged with driving under the influence. Despite all his success, he was depressed and wondering if life was worth living. Realizing he had been stuffing down his pain for too many years, Phelps checked into a rehab clinic and started opening up about his feelings.

Many high-profile athletes, like retired NHL goaltender Corey Hirsch and Dwayne "The Rock" Johnson, pro wrestler turned movie star, have started talking mental health. The common thread in these stories is that from the outside, each of these people look like they have it all. And yet success, wealth, good looks, magazine covers—you name it—don't necessarily insulate a person from mental health struggles. In fact, high levels of pressure and perfectionism can sometimes incubate emotional distress.

Lady Gaga, Prince Harry, Ariana Grande—the list of celebrities talking about their mental health goes on. They join the tide of everyday people transforming silence and shame into courage and openness.

Yayoi Kusama, a Japanese artist, creates brilliant, out-of-this-world paintings, sculptures and installations that are inspired by her own experience of hallucinations. Kusama had a traumatic childhood. Since 1977, she has resided in a psychiatric hospital, while still making and exhibiting her celebrated art.

BUSTING STIGMA

Stigma means a mark of disgrace or a stain. In the realm of mental health, stigma is negative judgments of others based in fear and ignorance. Stigma results in people being called "crazy" or "dangerous" or seen as failures.

In movies and TV shows, people living with mental illness are often portrayed as either out of control or completely zoned out. News stories about mental illness often focus on violent events and speculation about the person's mental state. It gets overlooked that people who have mental health challenges are more often the victims of violence. Stigma happens when the stereotypes blot out the complicated experiences and strengths of real people.

When someone has a heart attack or a stroke, it's taken seriously. And there's no shame in calling in sick for school or work. Friends and family rally around. Compassion and understanding are in good supply. But when someone is anxious or depressed, things can be more difficult. Instead of being treated with compassion, people sometimes get blamed for being weak or lazy. And when it's psychosis, the level of stigma can be even greater.

Stigma can stop people from asking for help. It can result in people suffering in silence.

The good news is that these attitudes are changing. Talking openly about mental health is one way to bust stigma.

Together we can create a society where asking for help is not a sign of weakness but a sign of strength. Here are a few more stories of people and organizations who are busting stigma in their lives and work.

UNDER ONE ROOF
INTEGRATED SERVICES FOR YOUTH

Hip-hop music and coloring books on the café tables. Splashy interior design with bright paint, chic lamps and phone chargers built into the couches. Friendly laughter and the smell of cherry Danishes wafting from the back kitchen. An Indigenous Elder smudging the Talking Room. This might not sound like the usual place you go when life takes a bad turn or your head gets topsy-turvy. This is Foundry.

It's not your typical doctor's office or counseling center or social services agency. There's no beige carpet or sterile waiting room. And yet you can see a doctor or find a counselor. You can get help with finding housing, getting a job, kicking an addiction or smoothing out family conflict. Plus there is cultural support, art therapy, cooking classes, trauma-sensitive yoga and much more. Foundry is a one-stop shop designed to help youth find wellness.

For too long, mental health services have been hard to access, especially for youth. So what gets in the way of people getting help? Well, there's a long list: services often are hard to find, are intimidating to walk into, and have really specific criteria you have to meet to be eligible or you're told to go elsewhere. Sometimes people don't want to be seen getting help because they're afraid of being judged.

WHILE MOST MENTAL HEALTH problems start in childhood or adolescence, research shows that only about 13 percent of youth actually try to access mental health services. And of the youth who do seek help, only about half get the services they need. Foundry is part of a wave of more accessible and holistic youth services worldwide. In Australia, headspace runs youth centers across the country and also offers a slick e-headspace with online counseling. In Ireland, Jigsaw operates in 10 different cities. These services have all made a point of consulting youth about what works for them and bringing multiple services together to work in an integrated way. Now California and Ontario have similar youth hubs in the works.

Foundry Campbell River is one of the first youth hubs to open in British Columbia, bringing a wide range of health and social services for young people up to age 29 under one roof so that they are easier to access. Now Foundry has 11 one-stop shops across BC. Each Foundry offers a chill waiting area. Peer support workers who "get it" are there to answer questions and help youth feel welcome.

Sometimes a youth may access mental health services, but without someone to give them a ride or bus money, they don't make it to the next appointment. Or if they don't have a safe place to live or good food to eat, it's tough to work on feeling better. Sometimes things get worse and worse until they end up in an ambulance or a police cruiser.

People with mental health struggles rarely have a single isolated problem. And rarely is there a single solution. When someone seeks out a counselor because they are feeling down, they may also need to see a doctor because they're not eating or sleeping well. They might need support with relationship troubles or finding a safe place to live. Or maybe help finding a job will be the thing that gives them a sense of purpose and a ticket to the next stage in their life.

At Foundry, all these services are in one place. A more holistic approach means that mental health supports go hand-in-hand with physical health, social connection, employment and many other aspects of well-being. When all these services are brought together, youth get comfortable and can flow from one service to another—without having to walk into another waiting room, without having to screw up the courage to try something totally new, and without having to tell their story over and over.

One of the big ideas is early intervention. The sooner you can get someone help, the more likely they'll recover quickly. If you treat illnesses or problems early, the whole population is healthier and health-care costs are lower. If youth are unwell during their teenage years, they can miss out on important learning and development, which may put them at a disadvantage for the rest of their life. This can make it difficult to get a good job or go to university. But when youth are helped to recover quickly, they can get back to learning and get on with living.

PEER SUPPORT

Andrea Vukobrat

Andrea Vukobrat knows that a big, warm smile can go a long way toward setting someone at ease. She started as a youth peer support worker at BC Children's Hospital and is now the peer support coordinator at Foundry Central. Peer support is all about youth drawing on their own lived experience to connect with other youth.

At first, Andrea was worried that because she had mental health challenges, she wasn't in a place to help others. But then she realized that *because* of her experience, she had a lot she could share.

TAKE A BREATHR

ANDREA SAYS THAT her counselor helped her to better understand the relationships between thoughts, feelings and actions. She now sees that her thoughts used to be very "all or nothing." Thoughts like: *If things don't go according to plan, then everything is ruined. If it's not perfect, then I'm a total screwup. If they're upset with me, I must be worthless and unlovable.* Andrea can now see that these thoughts weren't realistic or balanced and they drove her anxiety.

Andrea has practiced mindfulness meditation to help her observe her thoughts without necessarily believing they are true. Mindfulness is about being present in the here and now. Focusing on the breath while watching how thoughts spring up. You can practice not judging the thoughts and not latching onto them or spinning them into a story—but instead simply watch them float away like clouds drifting across the blue sky.

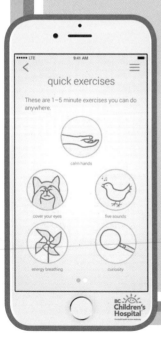

Mindfulness has been shown to reduce anxiety, depression and chronic pain. Brain scans show changes in brain structure, and people report feeling more positive and having a greater sense of calm and well-being after just eight weeks of regular meditation practice.

To learn more about mindfulness, check out the free Breathr app, which Andrea helped to develop, at **keltymentalhealth.ca/breathr**

Having worked on her own recovery, Andrea could offer practical tips and help youth navigate the system. As a young person, she could relate. She could understand. Most importantly, she could respond from a place of hope and inspire hope in others.

Many youth services now have peer support workers as part of the team. If a youth is feeling nervous about meeting a doctor or a psychiatrist, a peer support worker can go with them to the appointment. Or if filling out forms for social assistance or a name change is intimidating, a peer support worker can help figure it out. Sometimes it's just more comfortable to talk to another young person. Especially one who can say "I get it."

CULTURAL AND LAND-BASED HEALING FOR INDIGENOUS PEOPLES

Rennie Linklater is animated as she tells me about helping a friend make bear grease last summer. They took 60 pounds of bear fat, after the meat and fur had been removed, and boiled it down, strained it and put it in jars. "It's really, really strong medicine," Rennie says. "In Anishinaabe culture, the bear is one of our healers."

Rennie is a member of Rainy River First Nations in northwestern Ontario. She is also the director of Shkaabe Makwa at the Centre

Rennie Linklater

for Addiction and Mental Health (CAMH), a large psychiatric hospital based in Toronto and one of the world's leading mental health research centers.

Rennie draws from her Anishinaabe perspective to explain that culture is the foundation for wellness. Culture grows out of the land, language, traditions and history of a people. Ceremonies and cultural practices help to create balance in a person's mind, body, heart and spirit.

Many Indigenous communities hold cultural camps that help youth develop a positive identity and sense of belonging. Near Bella Bella, in the Great Bear Rainforest on the rugged northern coast of

British Columbia, Heiltsuk youth have the opportunity to attend the Koeye Camp each year, returning to a site on the Koeye River that their ancestors have known intimately for thousands of years. Here the youth gather foods and medicines, learn the Heiltsuk language and laws, and participate in Potlatch ceremonies. They also connect their traditional knowledge with environmental science so that they can continue to protect their lands for future generations.

Over the last 30 years cultural programs like the Koeye Camp have resulted in the youth suicide rate dropping dramatically in Bella Bella, BC.

Ilisaqsivik, a community organization in Clyde River, Nunavut, organizes camps for Inuit youth and their families. The Elders pass on traditional skills like sewing, tool making and running dog teams, while telling stories and giving teachings. Gathering on the land and enjoying food and laughter together helps people feel safe enough to talk about difficult topics. This is one way they are restoring their community and cultural connections.

In the Tairāwhiti community in Gisborne, New Zealand, Māori stories are transforming mental health services. Dr. Diana Kopua, a psychiatrist who is Māori, realized that the mainstream services weren't doing a good job of helping her people. So Dr. Di teamed up with her husband, Mark Kopua, who is a historian and tā moko tattoo artist, and they started Mahi a Atua, a narrative therapy with Indigenous roots in their tribal region.

Imagine a teenage boy who's anxious to even walk into the clinic and doesn't know how to find the words to begin to describe the bullying he's faced and how low he feels. Now imagine the room is full of Māori art, and instead of a stream of questions to zero in on what's wrong with him, he's greeted with stories of the atua, gods who are both powerful and flawed. His family and the health-care team gather around and join in the storytelling.

The stories are full of conflict and drama. The boy hears about Uru-te-ngārara, a god who was bullied by his younger brother and waded through loneliness and depression. The stories explore feelings like doubt, anger and remorse, and how to draw on creativity, courage and kindness. They open up a space to talk about difficult things and find a path out of the hard times.

Mahi a Atua literally means "tracing the ancestral footsteps of the gods." Dr. Di specializes in combining Western medicine and Māori healing. She says Mahi a Atua has resulted in fewer hospitalizations

Dr. Diana Kopua

Mark Kopua

MARK KOPUA, A TĀ MOKO ARTIST, noticed that many youth who don't feel comfortable accessing mental health services will walk through the doors of his tattoo studio and share their pain. Suicide rates among Māori youth are among the highest in the world. Tā moko is a traditional Māori sacred practice. Mark often works with people who are wanting to layer a tattoo over their visible or invisible scars. Mark believes the tattoos can help to transform pain into meaning. They are symbols of hope that can remind the person of their healing journey and their Māori identity.

and less reliance on medications. As Māori have suffered from colonization and intergenerational trauma, reconnecting with their own traditional stories can be comforting and strengthening.

In Toronto, Rennie Linklater has been working on bringing Indigenous healing practices into the hospital where she works so that Indigenous people can get care that fits with their cultural identity. At CAMH, Indigenous Elders and Healers are part of the care team.

As the first hospital in Ontario to run a sweat lodge at their ceremony grounds, culture is a significant part of the treatment services for First Nations, Inuit and Métis patients. There are specific areas in the hospital that are off the ventilation system so smudging ceremonies can take place. Bringing Indigenous cultural services into the hospital also helps educate non-Indigenous staff and doctors about how to interact with Indigenous patients in more respectful ways.

The ceremony grounds at CAMH include a sweat lodge, sacred fire and medicine gardens, where sage, cedar, sweetgrass and sacred tobacco are grown. Since opening in 2016, approximately 2,000 people have visited the ceremony grounds, and many have participated in full moon ceremonies, healing ceremonies, traditional cultural teachings, grieving ceremonies and naming ceremonies.

RENNIE'S STORY

Rennie dreams of bears—black bears, grizzly bears, white bears. This is a connection with healing spirits. "I understand that it's my destiny to heal," she says. "But it takes a lot of work."

Rennie pays close attention to her dreams. They are guides to her healing. A few years ago, she had a dream of a little baby who is lost and who no one is looking for. In the dream she felt frantic and stressed. Later that morning it dawned on her: "Oh, it's me. I'm the baby," she thought. "I'm the baby who's out in the world and nobody is looking for me." She realized that she needed to do this work of finding and taking care of herself.

Rennie sees trauma as an injury that happens to a person's spirit. Rennie herself has experienced many such injuries. At four months old, she was taken from her mother by the Children's Aid Society, placed in foster care and then adopted by a white family. This was part of the Sixties Scoop, a time when social workers swooped in to take Indigenous children from their families and communities and put them up for adoption. Like many children of this time, two generations of Rennie's family had attended Indian residential school. For Rennie, growing up in a white family without connections to her Indigenous culture was confusing and painful. Although she reconnected with her Indigenous family and community decades ago, the pain of loss continues to resurface in various ways. For example, government apologies for the harms done to Indigenous people can bring up difficult feelings that have been suppressed for years. This has been true for Rennie and many others.

Over the course of her life, Rennie has had two major "breakdowns" where she felt like she was falling to pieces. Her healing involved sorting through the pieces of her life experience and making decisions about how to put herself back together while leaving behind the painful pieces she no longer needed to carry with her. She reminds me that it can be helpful to think of these times as "breakthroughs" rather than "breakdowns." In order to heal, she needed to connect with those difficult memories and emotions. Painful times can bring about beautiful transformations.

During these breakthroughs, Rennie says she experienced terrifying emotions and suicidal thoughts, and at times she was able to see the spirit world and parallel realities. She believes that if she had been assessed by a psychiatrist, she would likely have been diagnosed with a number of DSM mental disorders and perhaps hospitalized. Instead, she turned to Anishinaabe healers and ceremonies.

"A lot of my work was about getting myself back into my body, because I was very dissociated," Rennie says. While the term *dissociation* comes from mainstream psychology, Rennie remembers first learning about it from an Anishinaabe Elder who described how, when someone gets really afraid, the spirit leaves the body. She sees dissociation as a protective response. Numbness and disconnection can be a way to survive.

And yet when people have the support to go into the pain—whether support from family and community, from cultural ceremonies or from doctors and counselors—the possibility of healing that pain can open up.

Rennie remembers a sweat lodge ceremony where a bear spirit came to help her. When it was her turn to speak, she felt the bear push her forward and she collapsed on the cedar covering the ground and began wailing. She could feel the medicine. It helped her go into that place of pain so she could heal it.

THE WE MATTER CAMPAIGN

A Tribe Called Red

n the *We Matter* videos, their stories are heart-wrenching. Their faces emotional and vulnerable. And their star power undeniable. In close-up shots, Indigenous celebrities share their difficult stories.

Kelvin & Tunchai

The hip-hop/pow-wow DJ crew A Tribe Called Red. Grace Dove, the Secwepemc actor who starred in The Revenant. Jordin Tootoo, the pro hockey player and Inuk from Rankin Inlet, Nunavut. These are just a few of the featured voices. Indigenous voices of hope, sharing what got them through painful times.

Within one month of launching, the We Matter social media campaign had over one million views. Then videos from Indigenous youth came pouring in. Youth speaking to other youth who need to hear some words of hope. Youth telling their stories and saying, "I matter, you matter, we matter."

Right around the time We Matter launched, the small Indigenous community of Attawapiskat, Ontario, was in the news because of 100 suicide attempts that had occurred over the short span of eight months. Kelvin and Tunchai Redvers, siblings and the cofounders of We Matter, grew up in Hay River, a small town on the shore of Great Slave Lake in the Northwest Territories. They are Dene and Métis. They remember what it was like to feel isolated and not know where to turn for help.

"Don't talk, don't trust, don't feel." Kelvin explains that this is what Indigenous children were taught in the Indian residential school system. And this was passed down to the next generations. His own grandmother attended the Fort Resolution Indian residential school. It was known as a harsh place, but she never spoke about it. She and the other children had been ripped from their communities and families, from their language and traditions. Showing emotion was punished. "That's just not human," Kelvin says. "We all need an outlet for expressing our emotions."

By the age of 15, Kelvin had found filmmaking. "That's how I got my stuff out. I was lucky. Not everyone has that." He poured his angst, anger and loneliness into his films. The shorts he made in high school went on

Sandy Lake First Nation

to win national and international awards, and now his films are screened at festivals around the world.

But many of Kelvin's cousins and other family members weren't so lucky. "I've lost so many people too soon," he says. To alcohol-related accidents, suicide and other tragedies. Kelvin's own sibling Tunchai experienced depression and brushes with suicide.

That's why Kelvin and Tunchai started the We Matter campaign. They wanted Indigenous youth to see positive Indigenous role models. They wanted to show that it's okay to talk about difficult feelings. They wanted youth to know that they were not alone.

Now when Kelvin and Tunchai put on workshops for Indigenous youth, it's the videos from other youth that are the most popular. The youth get it. They have creative ideas on how to survive and thrive. Their message of hope hits home.

You can check out the videos at **wemattercampaign.org** and join the #HopePact.

Joshua Watts

ON CULTURE, IDENTITY AND FINDING YOUR PURPOSE

"**HEY, MY NAME IS JOSH WATTS.** I'm Nuu-chah-nulth and I'm Coast Salish. I was born in Port Alberni and I grew up in Squamish, British Columbia. I came from a really low-income house and my family struggled with drug abuse. I moved out when I was 15 and went through my own problems and my own addictions.

How I overcame that is I took on my culture and I really took it in. I was searching for who I was. I was searching for my identity. The more I learned, the stronger I became. I started learning our songs. I started learning our dances. And I learned how to carve. The Squamish community really took me in. By participating in the culture and by learning the traditions and the teachings of our First Nations people, I began to find out who I was. I wasn't so lost anymore. And it was easier for me to find my purpose in life.

Today I go to university. In the future I want to be an environmentalist. I want to be involved with Indigenous law. It's never too late to find your purpose in life. It's never too late to grab onto something and work toward it every day to get you out of that dark spot, wherever you come from."

HERO BOOKS

Ten years ago when I arrived at Nekkies, I was driving a rickety 1970s VW Beetle. I had come to this small community in South Africa to volunteer with a youth group called MADaboutART. Once they got to know me, the kids would yell "vetkoek, vetkoek," their nickname for my car, which they thought looked like a hunk of deep-fried dough. They'd race barefoot alongside the lurching car or hitch a ride on the bumper as I drove to the community center.

At MADaboutART, 14-year-old Ebby hunches over his drawing. He has tuned out the buzz of the 12 other young people working on their pictures at a table strewn with markers and paint. His shoulders are slim, childlike. And yet his intent posture carries some of the energy of the more manly version of himself he has drawn.

In the drawing, Ebby has a wide-legged tough-guy stance and sports baggy jeans and a bulky down jacket—LA-rapper-style. He stands in front of a trim blue-and-red house in the mountains that looks like it could belong to the three bears.

He has left out the thousands of small shacks made of scraps of tin, plastic and dumped lumber that crowd the hillside here. Nekkies, the community Ebby calls home, is one of six townships surrounding the city of Knysna, one of South Africa's finest holiday destinations. Mansions, mostly owned by white people, sprawl along the sandstone cliffs that drop into the Indian Ocean. But in Nekkies, most of the residents are Black, and conditions are crowded and impoverished. Unemployment and HIV infection rates are among the highest in South Africa.

The youth at MADaboutART have worked with a narrative psychologist to write and illustrate their own stories. They've made books with cardboard covers and string binding. The idea is that by writing their stories, they can define their own problems in their own words. Through art and writing, they can explore their strengths and skills, and discover how they are so much more than the problem. They can also figure out some tricks and tactics to cope with the problem. They remember their shining moments and dream about who they will be in the future.

Currently, there are around 3.5 million orphans in South Africa, most of whom have lost one or both parents to AIDS. Many of these young people suffer from trauma but aren't able to access professional help. Making hero books is a simple, low-cost group activity that any school or community center can do to help youth understand their experiences and support one another.

When I first read Ebby's hero book, just the title—*Fix-it Super-hero*—had me hooked. Ebby wrote about when people shout at him and hurt him. He doesn't say who hurts him, but he has drawn a large

heart broken in two. "This feeling looks like a black dog, it sounds like a snake in the grass," he has written. "It feels like I'm locked up in jail. It smells like stinking eggs and tastes like old cake." Ebby calls it his monster. He grins at his shoes and half-dances with nervous energy when he talks about his monster. But he talks about it—to his grandmother, his auntie, his friends. Even just being able to talk about it can be helpful.

Young people from across the world have read the MADaboutART stories and then told their own stories. Nkosi, an 11-year-old from KwaZulu-Natal, South Africa, has written about ngiz izwa ngi nduvu nduvu—"to feel tired and sick, like sleeping." He wrote, "I am scared to be beaten and it feels like a snake with many heads." James, a 14-year-old from Malawi who has lived on his own since his parents died, wrote about "the helpless-hopeless, not-getting-up-the-whole-day, lack-of-support mountain" that makes it difficult for him to get to the market where he sets up his barber shop to make his own living.

At MADaboutART, the hero books are continual works in progress. As Ebby works on updating his book, he bops like a little elf with break-dancing moves. He knows that many kids in many different countries have been inspired to write their own stories after reading his book. Over top of the trees he writes, "I think my book will give a solution to those who have problems like me."

Even here in Nekkies, his friends treat him with respect because of the honesty in his book. One of Ebby's friends says, "Last time I wasn't that strong to put in what I wanted to put in. Now I want to make it more powerful." Here, it's become cool to talk about your feelings.

In the next room, seven other young people who are newer to MADaboutART are making hero books for the first time. When I ask if I can make my own book, three kids jump up to show me how to cut the paper and bind the cover. When I draw my problem, it's black and stormy. In the distance, a tiny red boat rides up an ominous wave-face. I call the problem "The Murky Drowning Sea." But the red boat looks like it might make it.

A few weeks later, working on the endings for our books. Ebby draws a square-shouldered version of himself in a sharp blue uniform, with crisp collars and tall lace-up boots. It's his best self—confident, smart, strong and compassionate. He wants to work as an undercover cop.

Making a hero book can help youth celebrate their smarts, their skills, their dreams. A hero book isn't magic. It's not a quick fix. It doesn't replace friends or family. It doesn't stop abuse or end sadness.

Yet these books have opened up a space of sharing and belonging. Someday, Ebby wants to make his township safe, as peaceful as his drawing with the snug home against the mountains. For now he has his story and the power to share it. On this page he has written *My book is the shelter of other kids.*

AUTHOR'S NOTE

AS I WAS sitting down to write the final paragraphs of this book, I got a text from a teen saying, "I'm crying right now. It's all too much." I called her, and I could hear the raw desperation in her voice. She'd bought some Xanax. She could end it all. People had betrayed her and everything was piling up. But she was willing to go to the hospital.

Everyone has a breaking point. I know I've been close to mine a few times.

My heart wanted to just envelop this kid with love and safety and acceptance. I wanted to say to her, *You're okay. You're worth it. You're a beautiful human being. And I want you to live and love and give the world the amazing gifts you have to give.* But she couldn't hear that.

She was hurting. Her spirit had been injured. Every bit of her—her mind, body, emotions and spirit—was hurting. It wasn't her fault. Life had given her a bunch of totally unfair things, plus a sensitive spirit that registers the pain so vividly.

I've got an inkling of what that feels like. I've got my own little red boat that sometimes feels barely afloat on the wild seas.

I'm so full of admiration for this struggling kid. It takes immense courage to be honest about the pain we're in and to ask for help. I'm monitoring my texts because I want to know for sure that she's made it to the hospital. Sometimes we need to be in a place where we're just kept safe. And then we can figure out the next steps.

Mental health is so complex. Every aspect of life factors in. The scientific study of our brains is ever advancing. And yet in so many ways, the things that make life worth living shimmer with mystery.

I hope these stories have shown you some of the many ways that people understand mental health and the many ways that people are working to respond with more compassion and understanding. Hopefully we can keep breaking down stigma and working toward a better society that supports people to be well, not just in body but in our emotions, our minds, our spirits.

If you are going through tough times, please don't forget that times of great difficulty can be times of great change and growth. And remember, we can all be a part of the movement toward wellness—with less judgment and more acceptance, less blame and more support, less shame and more love. We can each start within and then spread it around.

I hope these stories can be a place of refuge. Everyone suffers. Some more than others. But know that if you are feeling down, messed up, stressed out or unwell, you are not weird or unworkable. You are not alone. There is a way to get through this. I hope we can find it together.

ACKNOWLEDGMENTS

THIS BOOK WAS WRITTEN while I was living and working on traditional territories of the Songhees, Esquimalt and WSÁNEC peoples and the Nuu-chah-nulth and Kwakwaka'wakw peoples, on the beautiful island now known as Vancouver Island. I offer my respect for the living traditions and sovereignty of these nations and the knowledge they continue to hold about how to live with balance and vitality on this land.

I want to thank all the people who shared their stories and insights, especially Tina, Jeremy Dias, Nadia Gaffhari, Asante Haughton, Ebby Jonas, Diana Kopua, Mark Kopua, Susan Landell, Rennie Linklater, Jack Linklater Jr., the crew at MADaboutART, Rod McCormick, Shawn Pendenque, Kelvin Redvers, Tunchai Redvers, Dese'Rae L. Stage, Lee Thomas, Andrea Vukobrat, Lucas Todd Walters, Joshua Watts and Art Wlodyka. With vulnerability and courage, you have deepened my understanding and you have strengthened me in my own wellness journey. I know you do this for others too. I carry such gratitude also for all the youth who have been my teachers as we sit together to figure out how to make life worth living.

Thank you to those who generously shared their photographs and artwork. Thanks to the incredible team at Orca Book Publishers, who believe in the ability of young readers to take on difficult topics. I am so grateful to Sarah Harvey for being such a supportive and sharp editor. And thank you to Andrew Wooldridge, Ruth Linka,

Merrie-Ellen Wilcox, Kirstie Hudson, Audrey McClellan, Mark Grill and Belle Wuthrich for your work in making the book precise and snazzy.

Thank you to all my teachers through the years in writing, justice, decolonization, trauma work, counseling and being fully alive, especially Lorna Crozier, Lynne Van Luven, Lisa Mortimore, Mehmoona Moosa Mitha, Susan Strega, Yvonne Haist, Donna Jeffery, Gayle Ployer, Todd Ormiston, Joyce and Vic Underwood, Kirsteen Moore, Iris Elsdon, Lori McKeown and Stacy Folk.

Thank you to my family for walking the difficult times with me. You are such examples of what it means to live with thoughtfulness and compassion. Thank you to Rob Skelly and Anne-Marie Turza for close readings, sparkling conversations and continual support. Thank you to Ali Blythe for being with me in this from beginning to end. Love to you all.

RESOURCES

INTEGRATED YOUTH SERVICES

allcove (United States): *allcove.org*

Foundry (Canada): *foundrybc.ca*

headspace (Australia): *headspace.org.au*

Jigsaw (Ireland): *jigsaw.ie*

Youth Wellness Hubs Ontario (Canada): *youthhubs.ca/en*

MENTAL HEALTH INFORMATION

Active Minds: *activeminds.org*

American Psychiatric Association: *psychiatry.org/patients-families*

Centre for Addiction and Mental Health: *camh.ca/en/health-info*

Heads Above the Waves: *hatw.co.uk*

HeretoHelp: *heretohelp.bc.ca*

Kelty Mental Health Resource Centre: *keltymentalhealth.ca*

Mind: *mind.org.uk*

mindyourmind: *mindyourmind.ca*

OK2TALK: *ok2talk.org*

On My Mind: *annafreud.org/on-my-mind*

STEPP: Vers la Santé Mentale: *stepp.ca/home.php*

TeenMentalHealth.org: *teenmentalhealth.org*

The Mighty: *themighty.com*

TOPIC-SPECIFIC RESOURCES

Anxiety
Anxiety Canada: *anxietycanada.com*

Depression
Bounce Back: *cmha.bc.ca/programs-services/bounce-back*

Youth Beyond Blue: *youthbeyondblue.com*

Eating Disorders

Kelty Eating Disorders:
keltyeatingdisorders.ca

Indigenous Youth

Centre for Native American Youth: *cnay.org*

Connect with Culture: *cultureforlife.ca*

We Matter: *wemattercampaign.org*

Recovery

Food for Thought: A Youth Perspective on Recovery-Oriented Practice (Video by the Youth Council of the Mental Health Commission of Canada): *mentalhealthcommission.ca/ English/media/3975*

Schizophrenia

Schizophrenia Society of Canada: *schizophrenia.ca*

Self-Injury

Self-Injury Outreach and Support: *sioutreach.org*

Sexualized Assault/ Gender-Based Violence

Project Respect: *yesmeansyes.com*

Substance Use Issues

Kelty Mental Health: *keltymentalhealth.ca/substance-use*

Cannabis and Psychosis: *cannabisandpsychosis.ca*

Suicide Prevention

Live Through This: *livethroughthis.org*

Now Matters Now: *nowmattersnow.org*

Transgender Health

Trans Care BC (Canada): *phsa.ca/transcarebc*

Rainbow Health Ontario (Canada): *rainbowhealthontario.ca*

Trauma

The Impact of Sexualized Violence: *vsac.ca/impact*

Trauma: *pamf.org/teen/life/ trauma*

What Is Complex Trauma?: A Resource Guide for Youth and Those Who Care about Them: *nctsn.org/resources/what-complex-trauma-resource-guide-youth-and-those-who-care-about-them*

GLOSSARY

addiction—the inability to stop using a substance or doing an activity that has negative long-term consequences, because it provides a short-term reward

anorexia nervosa—an eating disorder characterized by an extremely low body weight and a distorted body image

anxiety—feelings of nervousness and fear, which may be accompanied by worried thoughts, shallow breathing, a rapid pulse, stomach ache, tense muscles and restlessness

attention deficit hyperactivity disorder (ADHD)—a mental health diagnosis characterized by difficulties with paying attention or hyperactivity, or with both

binge eating disorder—an eating disorder characterized by a pattern of eating large quantities of food quickly and often with a feeling of being out of control

bipolar disorder—a mental health diagnosis characterized by cycles of depressed moods and elevated moods

bimarstan—a Persian word that means "hospital"

borderline personality disorder—a mental health diagnosis characterized by intense, reactive moods, a fragile sense of self, difficulties in relationships and impulsive behavior

brain stem—the part of the brain that regulates many basic functions of living, such as breathing, heart rate, sleeping and the activity of the central nervous system

bulimia nervosa—an eating disorder characterized by a pattern of eating a large amount of food quickly and then doing things like throwing up, fasting or exercising excessively

danger to self or others— a concept that can be used to legally restrict a person's freedom based on the prediction that they are likely to hurt themselves or someone else if they are not hospitalized or treated against their will

delusion—a firmly held belief in something that isn't true

depression—a common mental health diagnosis characterized by feelings of sadness, emptiness or irritability, along with feeling hopeless, worthless or guilty

dissociation—an experience of being disconnected from the here and now, often in response to a traumatic event or reminder; dissociation can range from feeling mildly spaced out or unreal to completely blanking out and losing time

DSM—the *Diagnostic and Statistical Manual of Mental Health Disorders*; describes over 300 different conditions and their symptoms

emotional brain—combined, the brainstem and the limbic area of the brain are sometimes referred to as the "emotional brain," the part of the brain that can react instantaneously to danger in order to keep us safe

fight, flight or freeze— the body's automatic stress response to real or perceived danger

generalized anxiety disorder—a mental health diagnosis characterized by persistent high anxiety that is difficult to control and out of proportion to the stressors

hallucination—an experience of perception when there is actually nothing to perceive (for example, hearing voices)

harm reduction—an approach to substance use treatment that emphasizes practical strategies to help a person decrease their use, or use in safer ways, and recognizes that total abstinence isn't realistic or desirable for many people

Indigenous—the original inhabitants and caretakers of a given territory. In Canada this includes the distinct societies of First Nations, Inuit and Métis Peoples

intoxication—when a person's thoughts, feelings and behaviors are altered by the use of drugs or alcohol

lack of insight—a cognitive deficit that prevents some people who experience psychosis from understanding their symptoms or realizing that they are ill

LGBTQ2S+—an abbreviation for Lesbian, Gay, Bisexual, Transgender, Queer, Two-Spirit plus other sexual and gender identities that tend to be marginalized

limbic brain—sometimes called the mammalian brain, the limbic brain is composed of many parts located deep in the center of the brain, including the hypothalamus and amygdala. The limbic system is involved in creating and regulating our emotional responses

mania—a mental state characterized by a heightened mood that is either euphoric or irritable and lasts for at least a week—symptoms include an unrealistic sense of superiority, hyperactivity, racing thoughts, pressured speech, sleeplessness and risky or excessive behavior

mental disorder—often used interchangeably with *psychiatric disorder* and *mental illness*; a health condition that involves changes in a person's emotions, thoughts and behaviors that cause them distress or make it difficult for them to function in daily life

mental health—describes a person's sense of well-being and ability to manage their thoughts, feelings and behaviors

mental health professional—person trained to work in the mental health field; includes doctors, psychiatrists, nurses, psychologists, social workers, psychotherapists, occupational therapists and others

mental illness—often used interchangeably with *mental disorder*

mood disorder—a group of mental disorders in which the main symptom is a disturbance in the person's mood

neocortex—the outer layer of the brain, which is especially well-developed in humans as compared to other mammals. The neocortex is the part of the brain that gives us the capacity to analyze facts and experiences, to imagine and create, to think before we act, and to manage complex thoughts about the self, our relationships and how to act wisely and ethically

neurotransmitters—the chemical messengers of the brain, such as dopamine, serotonin and epinephrine

obsessive-compulsive disorder (OCD)—a mental health diagnosis characterized by unwanted, irrational and disturbing thoughts (obsessions) and repetitive acts (compulsions)

panic attack—an experience of intense fear that comes on suddenly and includes physical symptoms of stress, such as a pounding heart, shortness of breath, trembling, nausea, dizziness, numbness or tingling in the hands and feet, and chest pain

panic disorder—a mental health diagnosis characterized by recurrent but unexpected panic attacks and avoidant behavior in hopes of preventing further panic attacks

post-traumatic stress disorder (PTSD)—a psychological injury caused by exposure to one or more traumatic events, such as acts or threats of violence, sexualized abuse, car accidents, war or natural disasters

psychoanalysis—a form of talk therapy, originally developed by Sigmund Freud, that explores a person's dreams, fantasies and free associations in the hope of bringing unconscious conflicts into the light of consciousness

psychosis—a condition in which a person's mind loses contact with reality; along with delusions and hallucinations, a person may also experience dulled emotions, difficulty relating to others, trouble thinking clearly and odd speech patterns

psychotherapy—talk therapy that can be conducted one-on-one or in a group setting with a counselor or therapist

recovery—in the field of mental health, a state where a person achieves greater self-determination and is able to create a purposeful, hopeful life even though they may still live with some of the symptoms of mental illness; in the area of substance use, a journey toward living a fulfilling life without relying on substances, with a recognition that relapse is sometimes a part of the recovery journey

schizoaffective disorder—a mental health diagnosis characterized by hallucinations or delusions in addition to a major mood episode, either depressive or manic

schizophrenia—a mental health diagnosis characterized by hallucinations, delusions and/or incoherent speech, as well as negative symptoms, such as decreased motivation and emotional expression

self-injury—he intentional injuring of one's own body, often as a coping strategy to seek relief

from intense feelings or emotional numbness

sexualized abuse—physical or psychological violence carried out through sexualized acts; includes any unwanted contact or harassment that targets sexuality

social anxiety disorder—an anxiety disorder in which a person is anxious about social situations because they fear they will be judged, humiliated or rejected by others

stigma—unfair judgement based on negative stereotypes

substance abuse—the problematic use of a substance that affects a person's health, work, school, relationships or other aspects of daily life in a negative way

substance use disorder—a mental health diagnosis where drug use has created changes in the brain's structure that result in intense cravings and repeated relapses, despite a desire to cut down or quit, and leads to an impaired ability to function in daily life

suicidal thoughts—experiencing thoughts about wanting to die, with or without the intent to die by suicide

therapist—a professional who provides psychotherapy (talk therapy) for people experiencing mental health problems and emotional difficulties; psychotherapy can be provided by psychiatrists, psychologists, social workers, clinical counselors, nurses and others with training

trauma—a physical or psychological injury; in the case of psychological injury, a response to a frightening or awful event that affects a person's body, mind, emotions and spirit

trauma triggers—external (sights, sounds, smells, etc.) or internal (thoughts, memories, sensations, etc.) reminders of a traumatic event that cause the body to go into a fight, flight or freeze response

withdrawal—a bodily response that occurs when a person stops using a substance that the brain has gotten used to, such as alcohol, drugs or prescription medications

PHOTO CREDITS

CHAPTER THREE

p. 61: Igor Madjinca/Stocksy.com; p. 63: Katarina Radovic/Stocksy.com; p. 65: Leonard Mc Lane/Getty Images; p. 66 Vitaliy Smolygin/Dreamstime.com; p. 68: American Philosophical Society; p. 69: Superbass/Wikimedia Commons (CC BY-SA 4.0); p. 71: Museum of the City of New York. Photo Archives. X2010.11.9957; p. 73: Ian S./Geograph UK (CC BY-SA 2.0); p. 76: Roman Bodnarchuk/Shutterstock.com; p. 79: Matthew Sherwood and the National Post; p. 80: Alan Budman/Alamy.com; p. 82: New Westminster Police Department

CHAPTER FOUR

p. 87: fizkes/Shutterstock.com; p. 89: Victor Torres/Stocksy.com; p. 92 (center left): Fabio Diena/Shutterstock.com; p. 92 (bottom right): Everett Collection/Shutterstock.com; p. 95: Bradley Parker; p. 96: Shilo McCavour; p. 99: August Natterer [Public domain]/Wikimedia Commons; p. 101: Hayden Williams/Stocksy.com; p. 102: courtesy of Unity; p. 105: Roxana Gonzales/Shutterstock.com; p. 107: Westend61/Getty Images; p. 109: Cristian Negroni/Getty Images; p. 110: courtesy of Vancouver Coastal Health; p. 113: bbernard/Shutterstock.com; p. 117: martin-dm/Getty Images; 122: Vince Lattanzio; p. 123: Rawpixel.com/Shutterstock.com

CHAPTER FIVE

p. 127: Hero Images/Getty Images; p. 130: Guille Feingold/Stocksy.com; p. 132: Remí Thériault; p. 134: Portrait by Stephanie Cardoso; p. 139: courtesy of Stella's Place; p. 140: Nipitphon Na Chiangmai/EyeEm/Getty Images; p. 141: Gawrav Sinha/Getty Images; p. 143: skynesher/Getty Images

CHAPTER SIX

p. 146: DFree/Shutterstock.com; p. 147: Andrew Toth/Getty Images; p. 149: courtesy of Foundry; p. 150: Jeff LeDrew; p.151: courtesy of Andrea Vukobrat; p. 152: BC Children's Hospital (keymentalhealth.ca/breathr); p. 153: Nadia Green/CAMH; p. 154: QQS Projects Society; p. 156: courtesy of Dr. Diana and Mark Kopua; p. 157: Miguel Amante/CAMH; p. 159: A Tribe Called Red; p. 160: Rhonda Dent; p. 161: courtesy of We Matter; p. 162 (top): YVRART Foundation; p. 162 (bottom right): Kris Krug; p. 163: courtesy of Melanie Siebert; p. 165: courtesy of Melanie Siebert; p. 167: Rob Skelly

Every effort has been made to locate and credit the correct copyright owners of the images used in this book. The publisher apologizes for any errors or omissions and would be grateful if notified of corrections that should be made in future reprints or editions.

INDEX

CONTINUE THE CONVERSATION

Kirkus' Best Books of 2019
SLJ Best Books 2019

9781459817128

"Required reading for
teens of every gender."
—*Booklist*, starred review

"A boon for those seeking clear,
comprehensive information."
—*Kirkus Reviews*, starred review

MONIQUE POLAK

9781459818927

"Fascinating and
passionately written."
—*Canadian Children's Book
News*, starred review

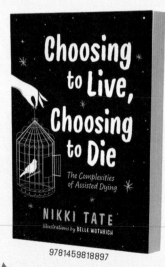

9781459818897

"A fascinating guide."
—*School Library Journal*,
starred review

**SUBJECTS THAT ARE AS PERSONAL
AS THEY ARE POLITICAL.**